This Book Belongs To

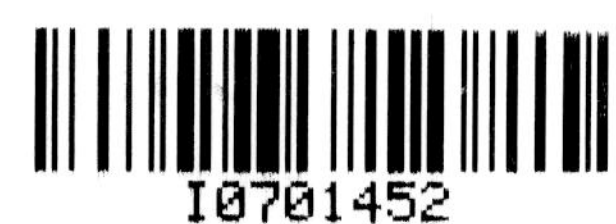

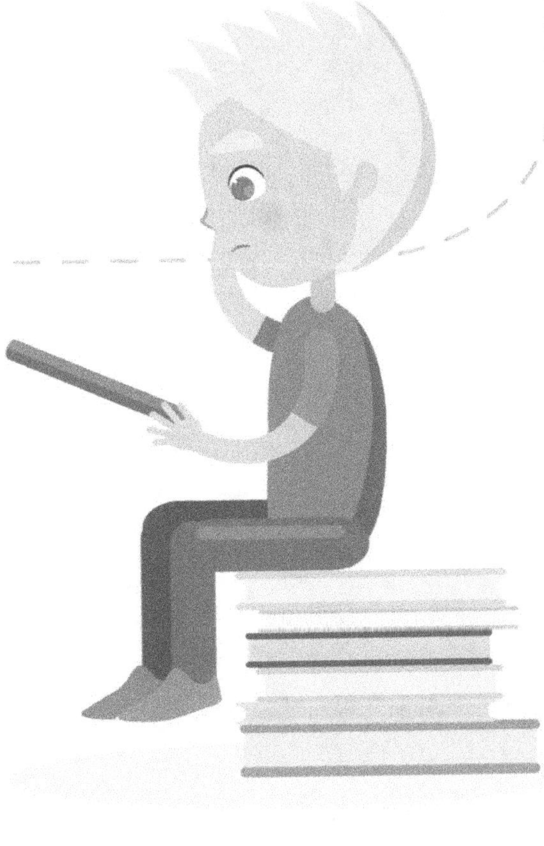

Color Test Page

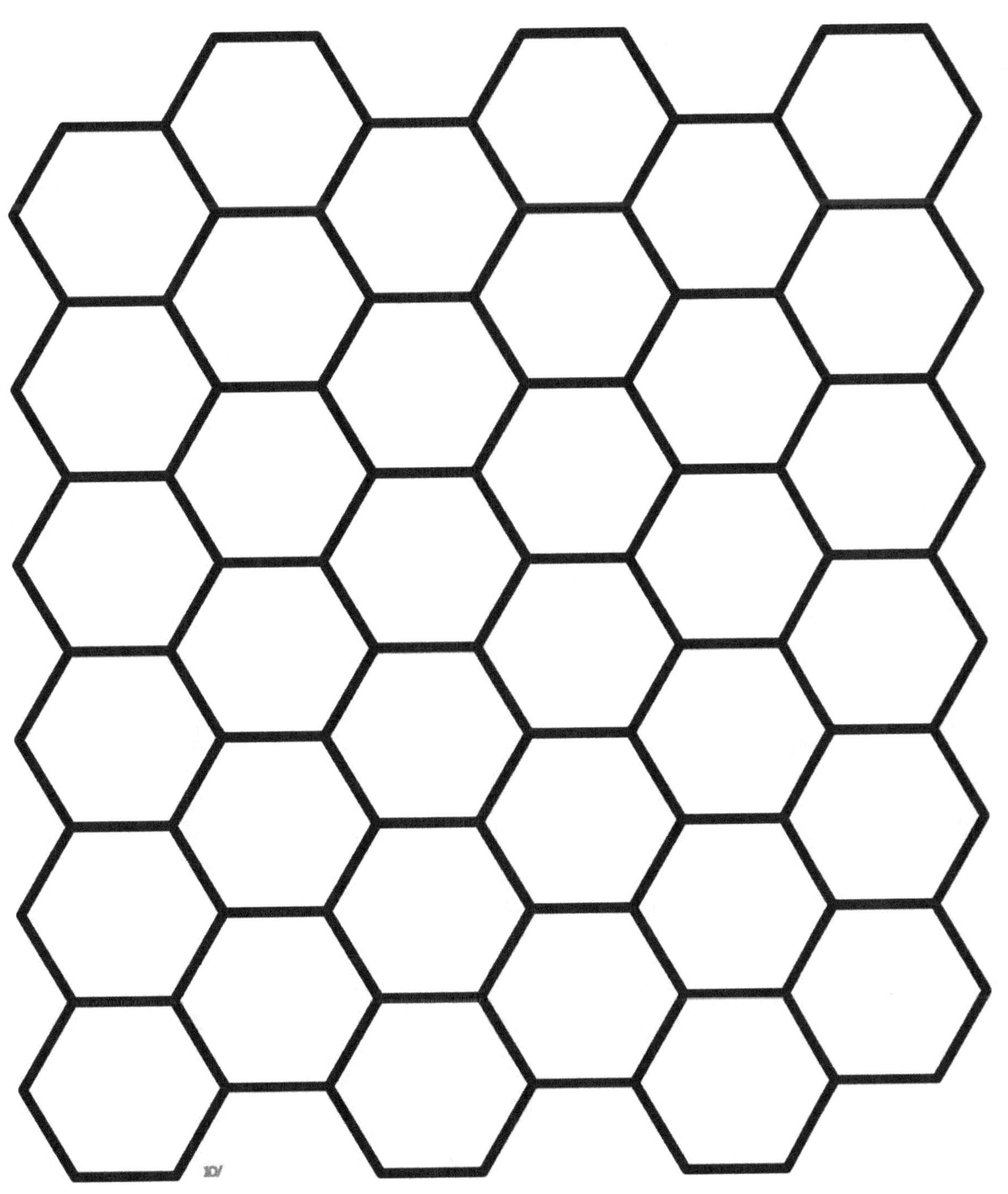

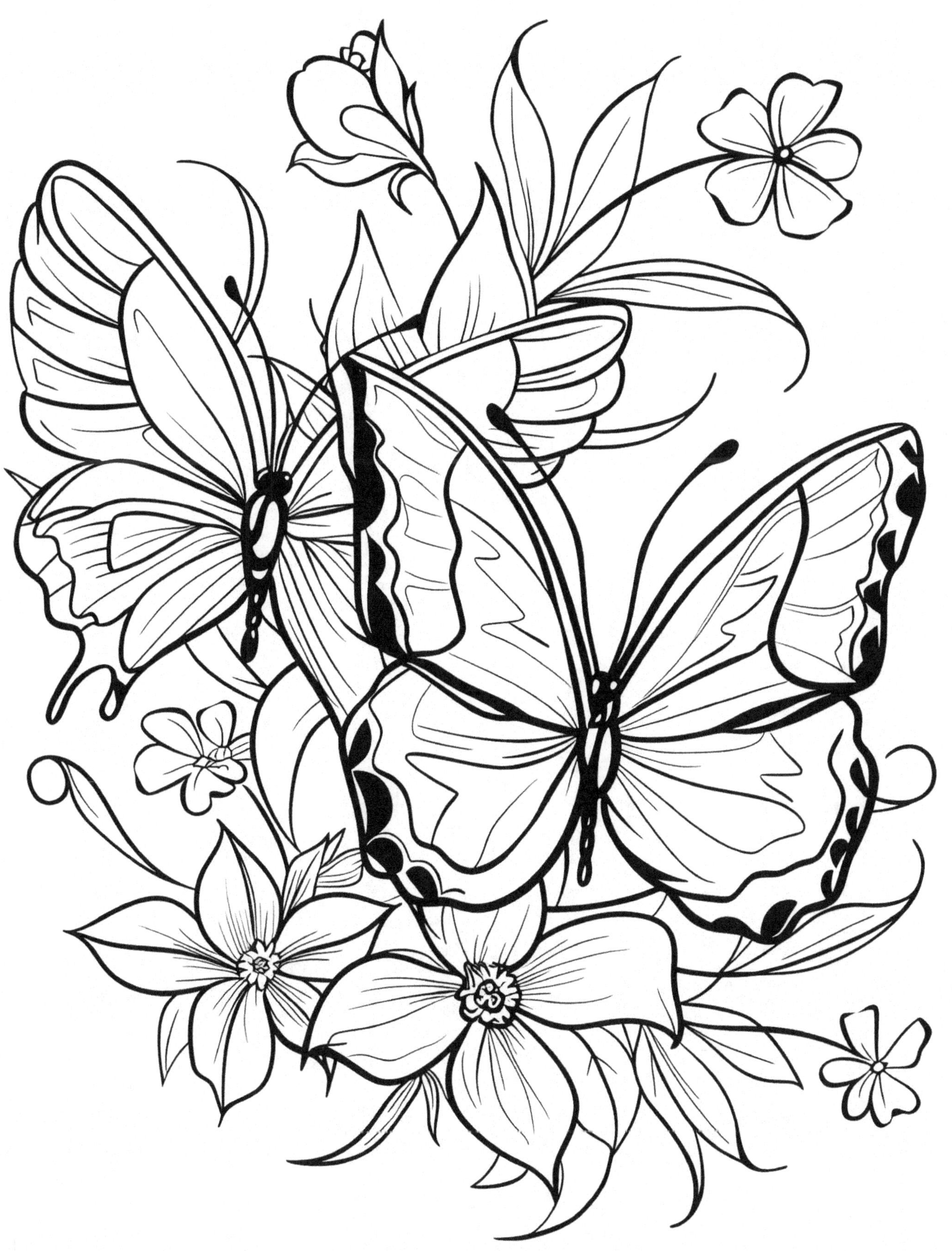

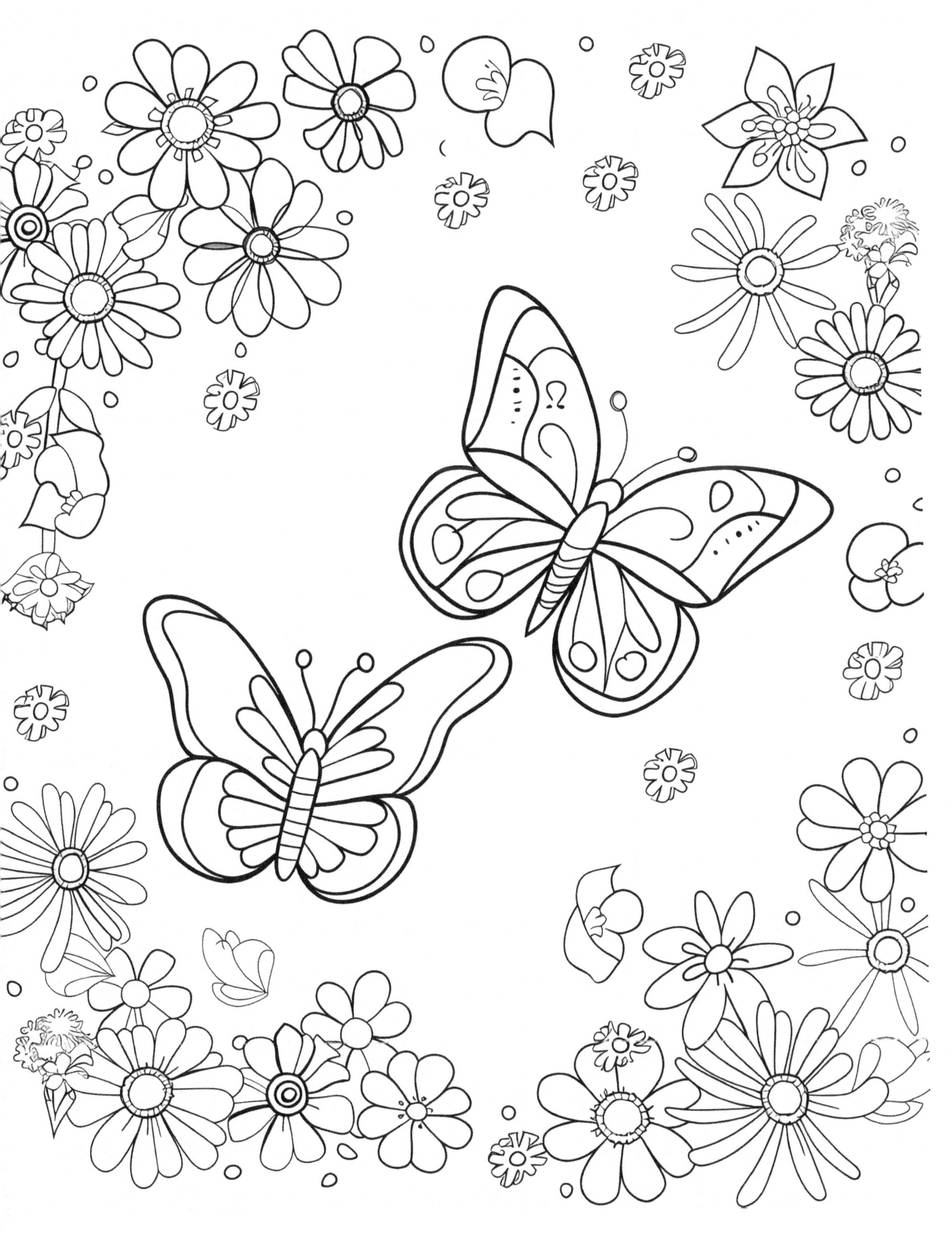

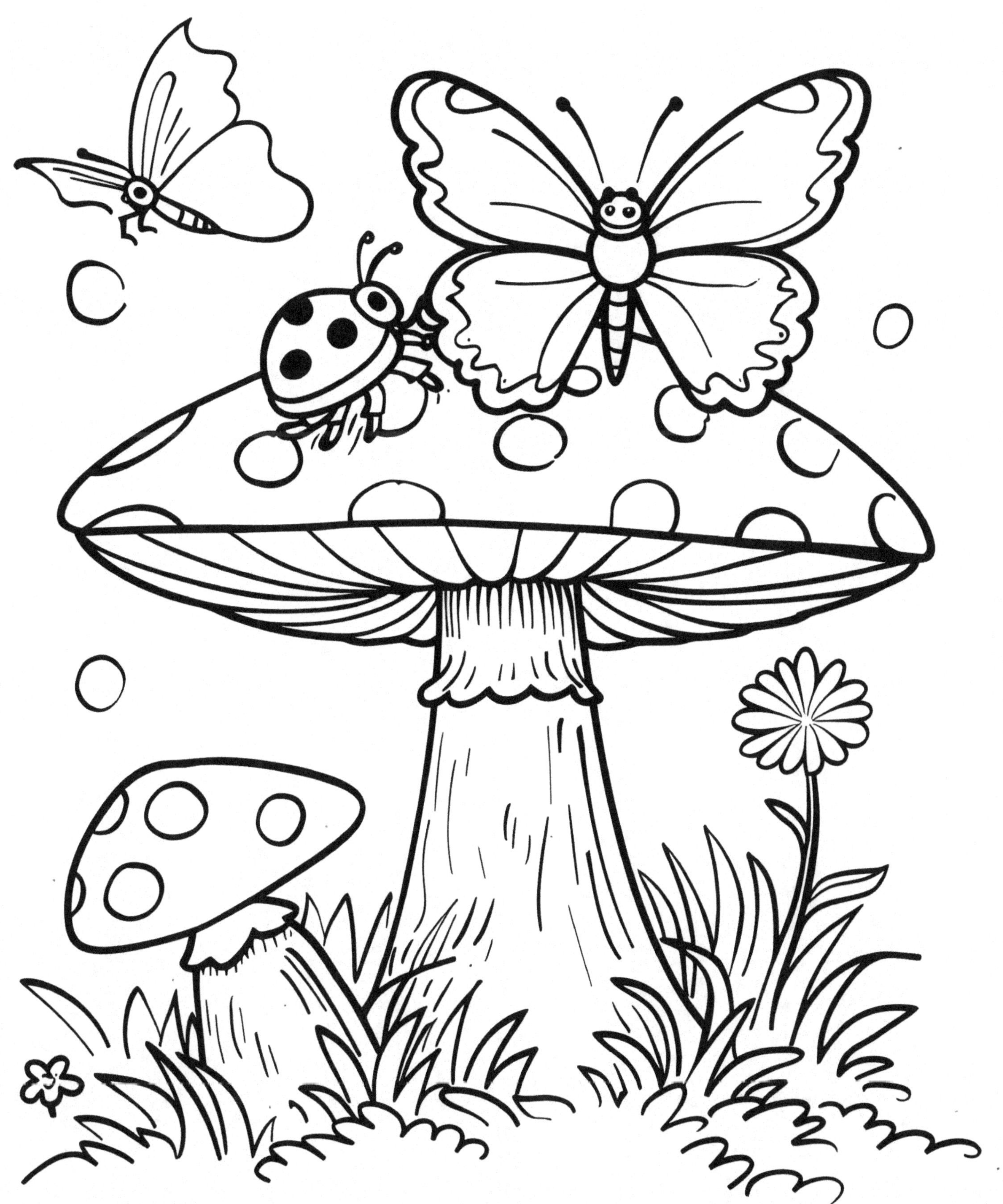

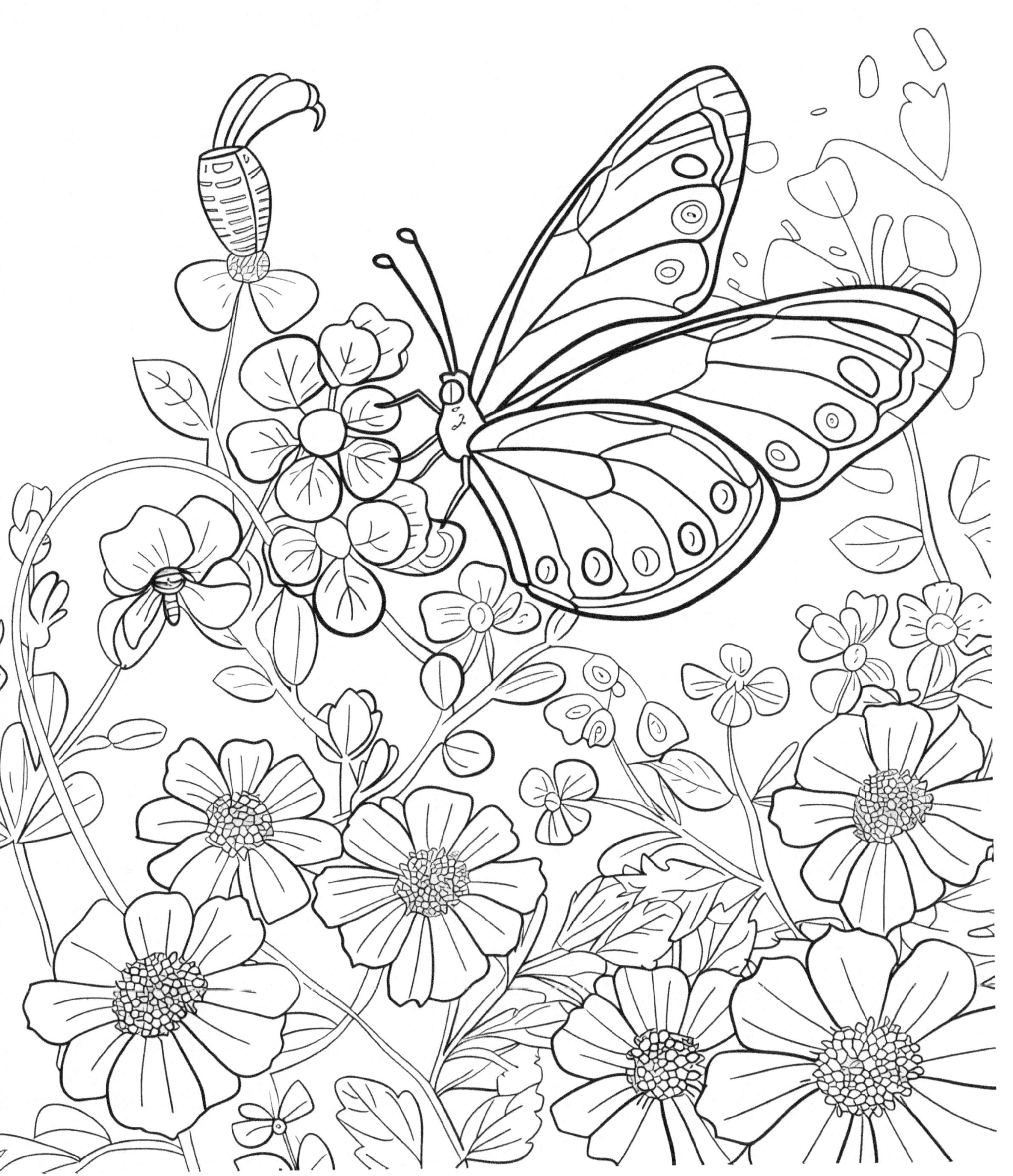

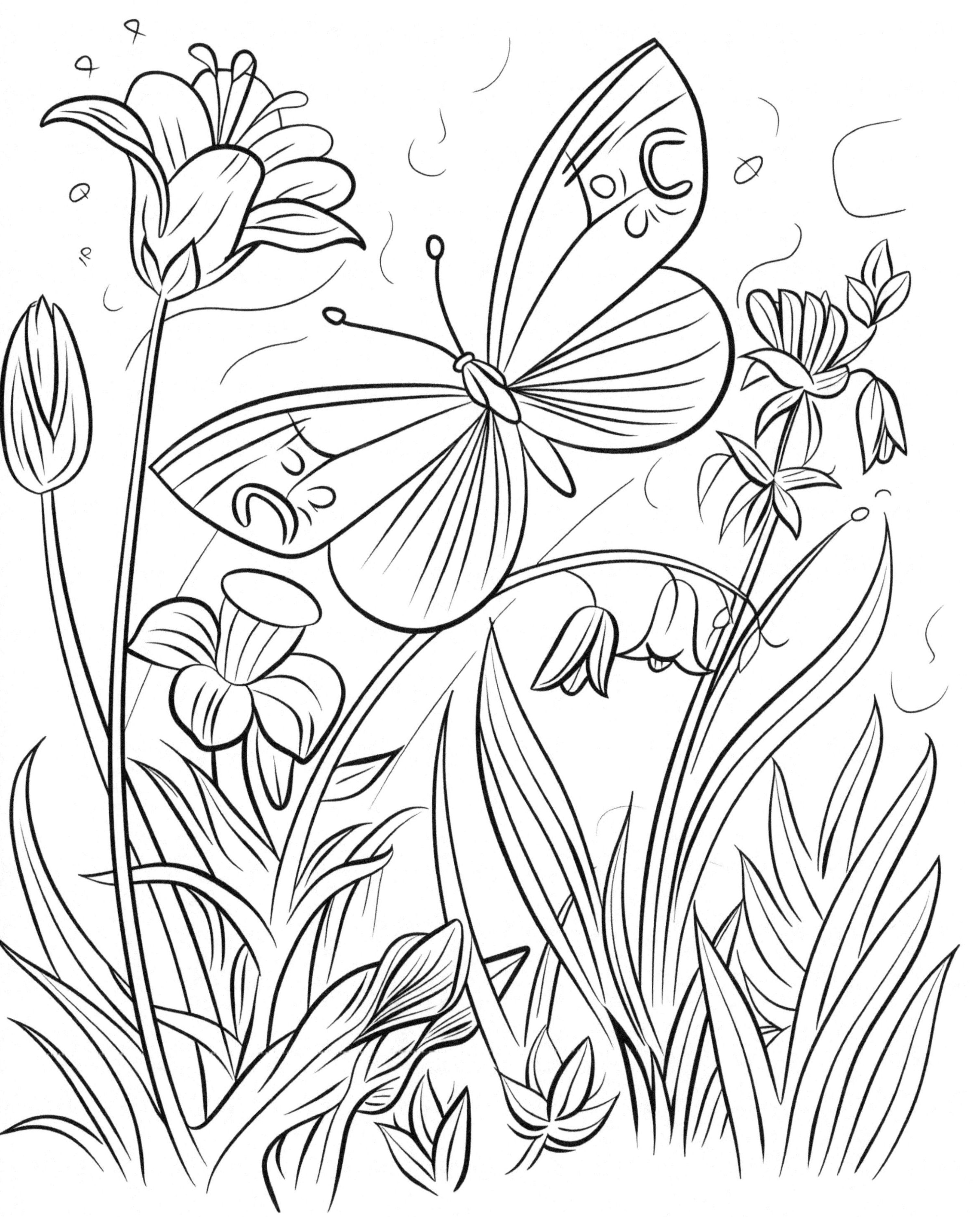

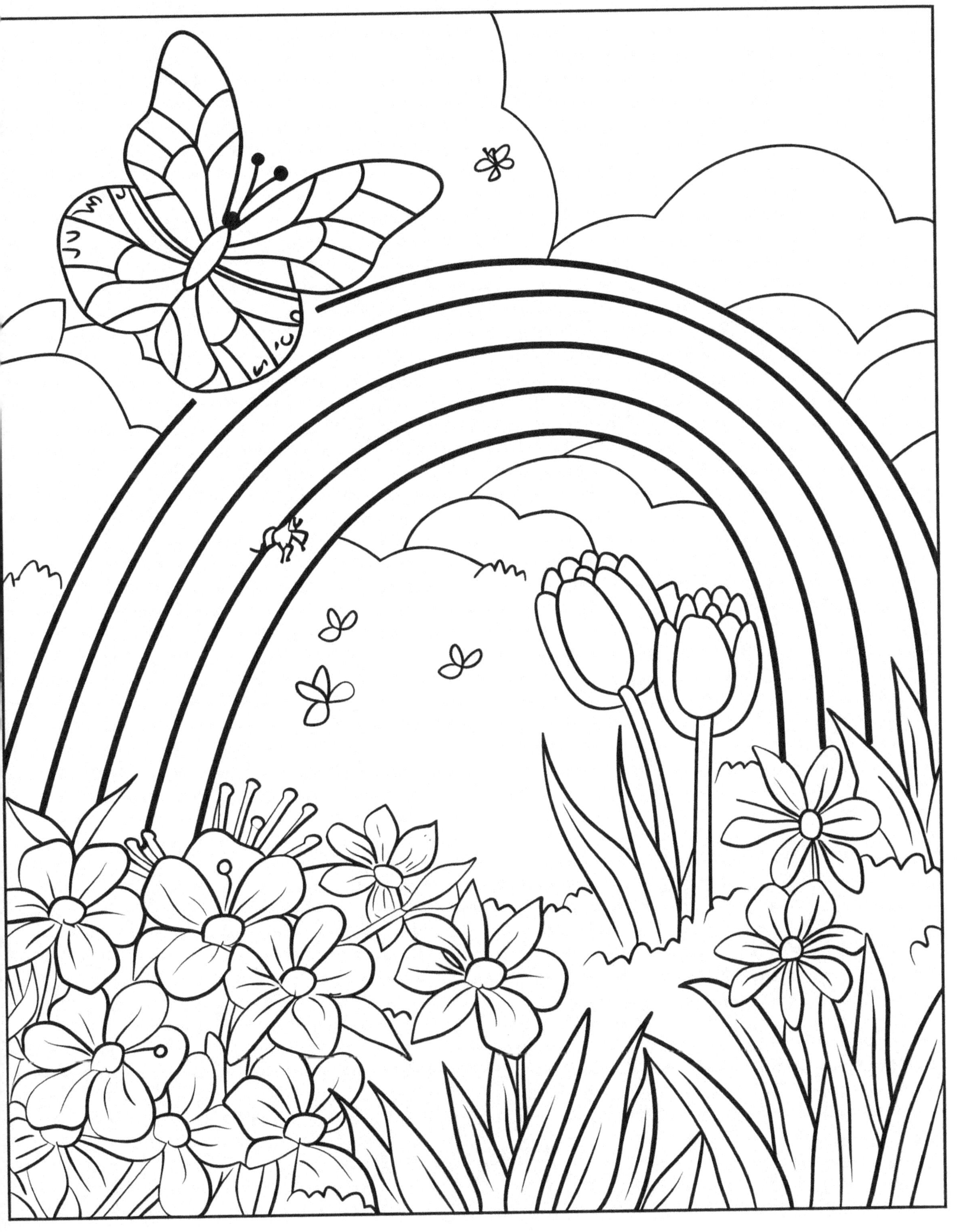

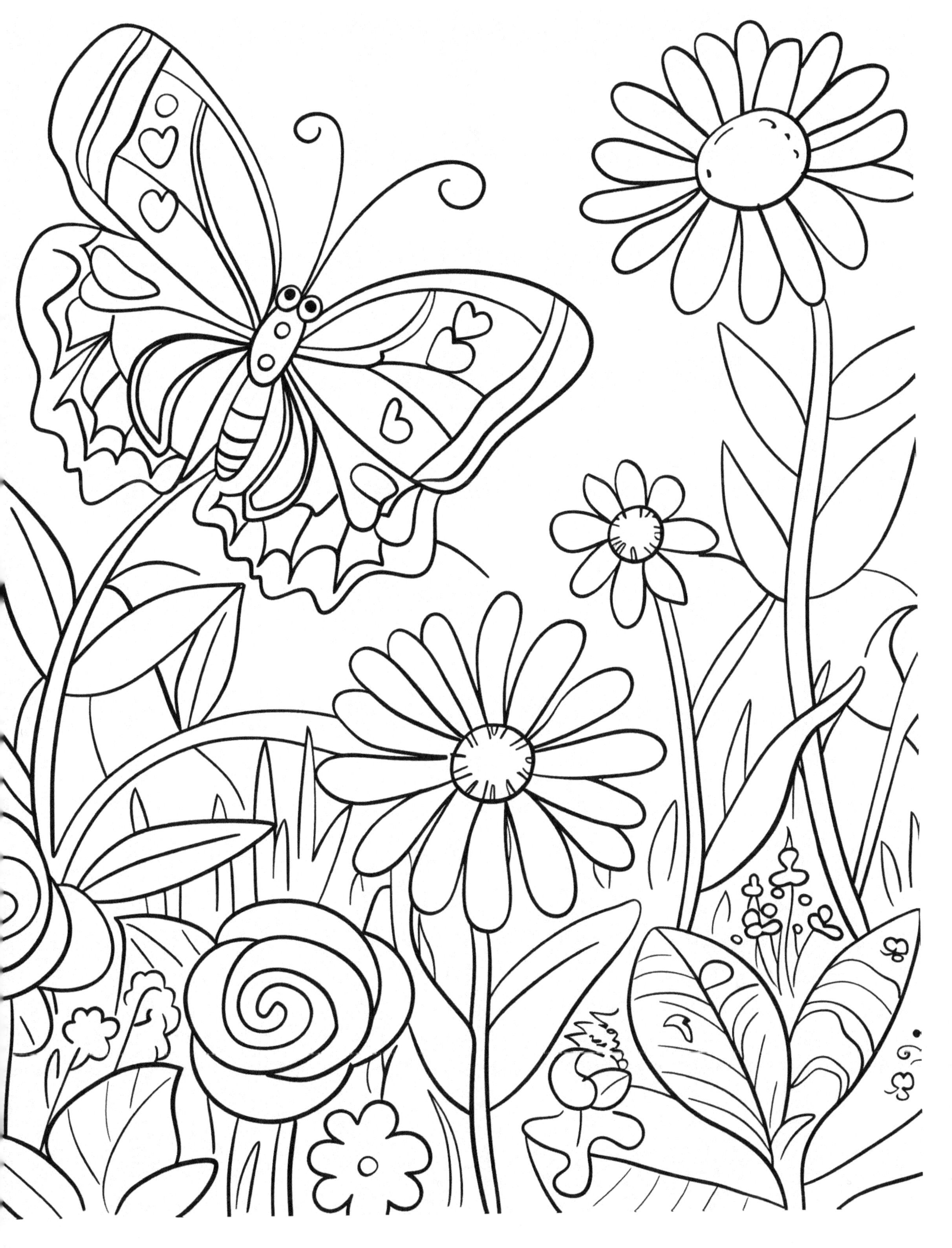

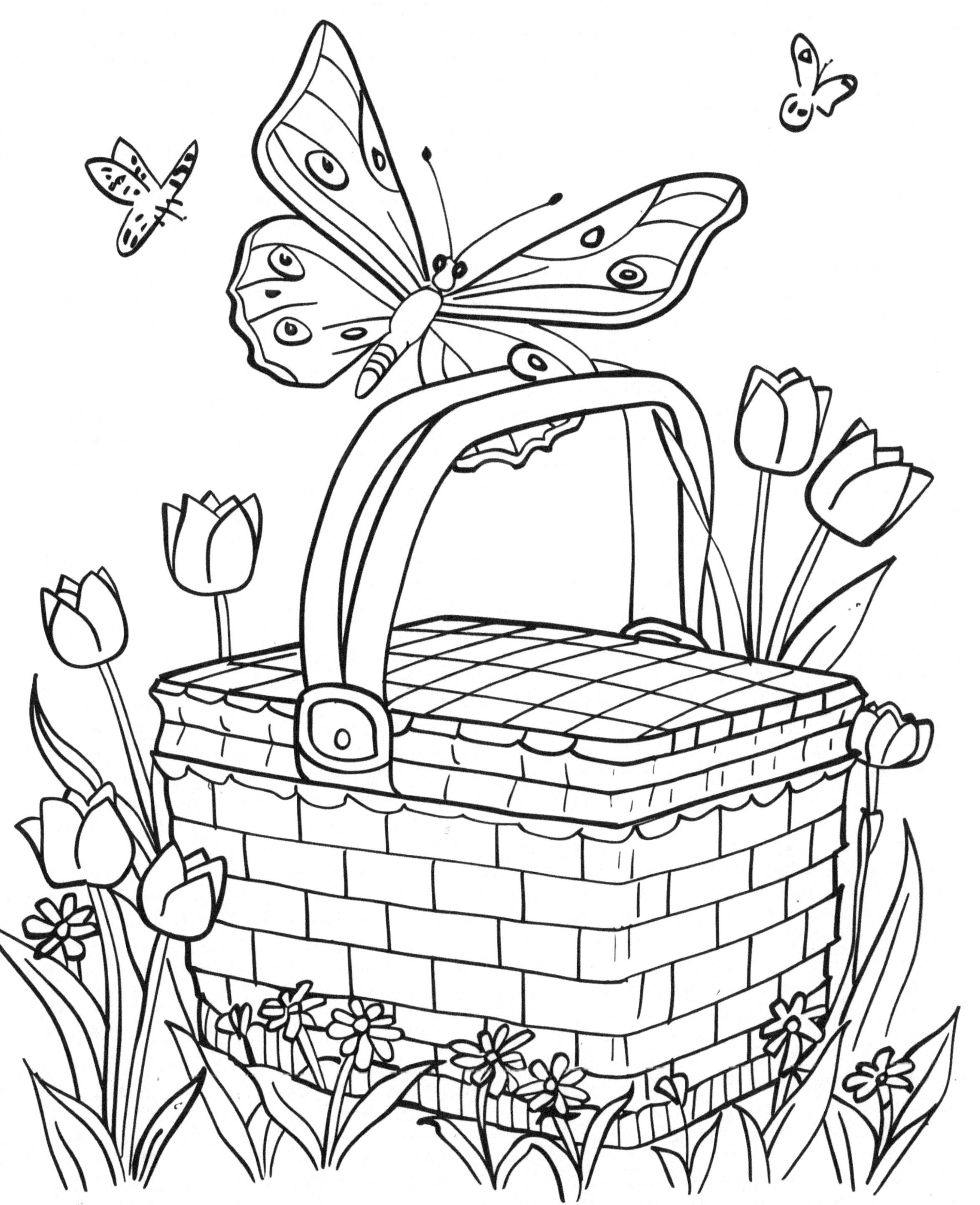

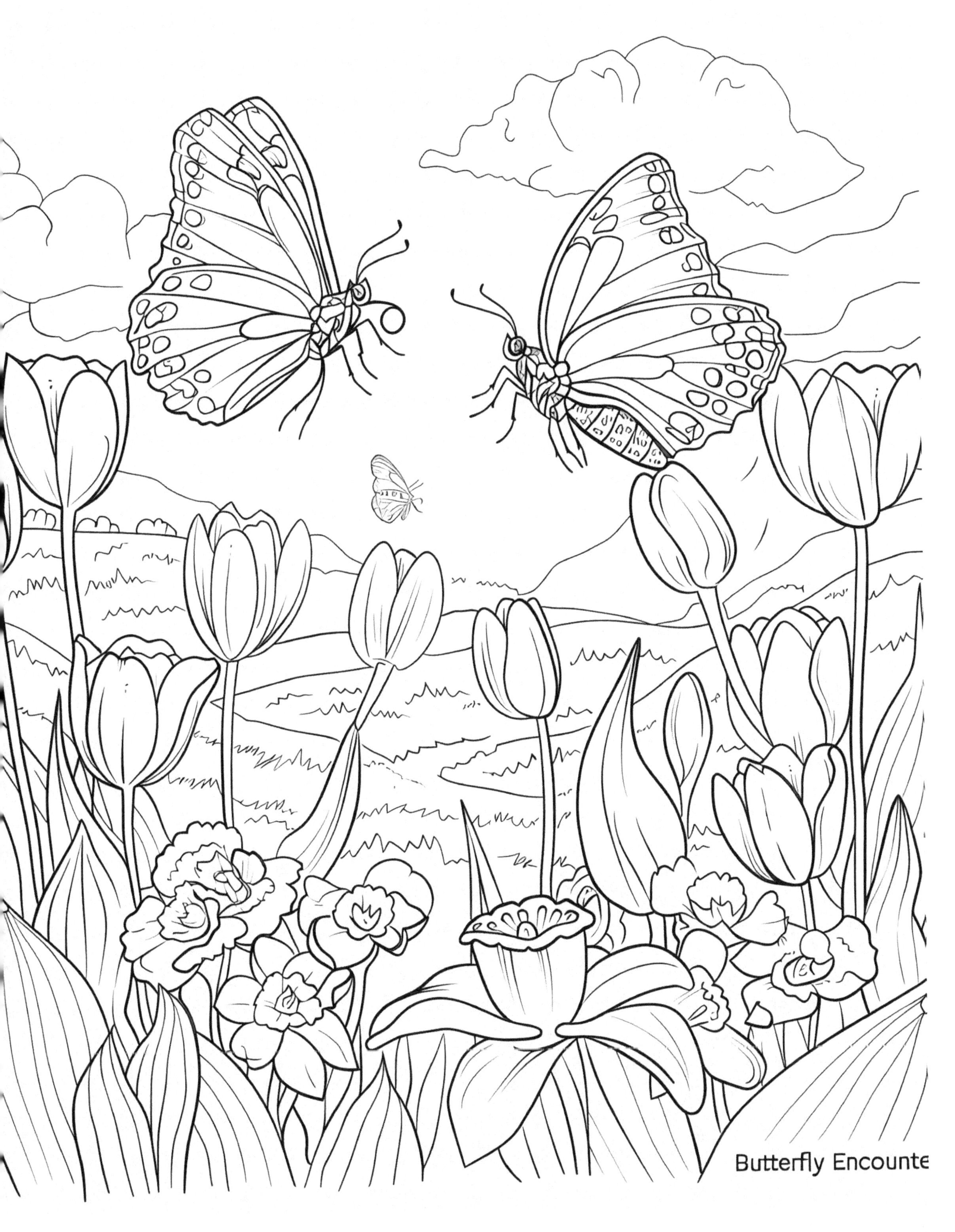
Butterfly Encounte

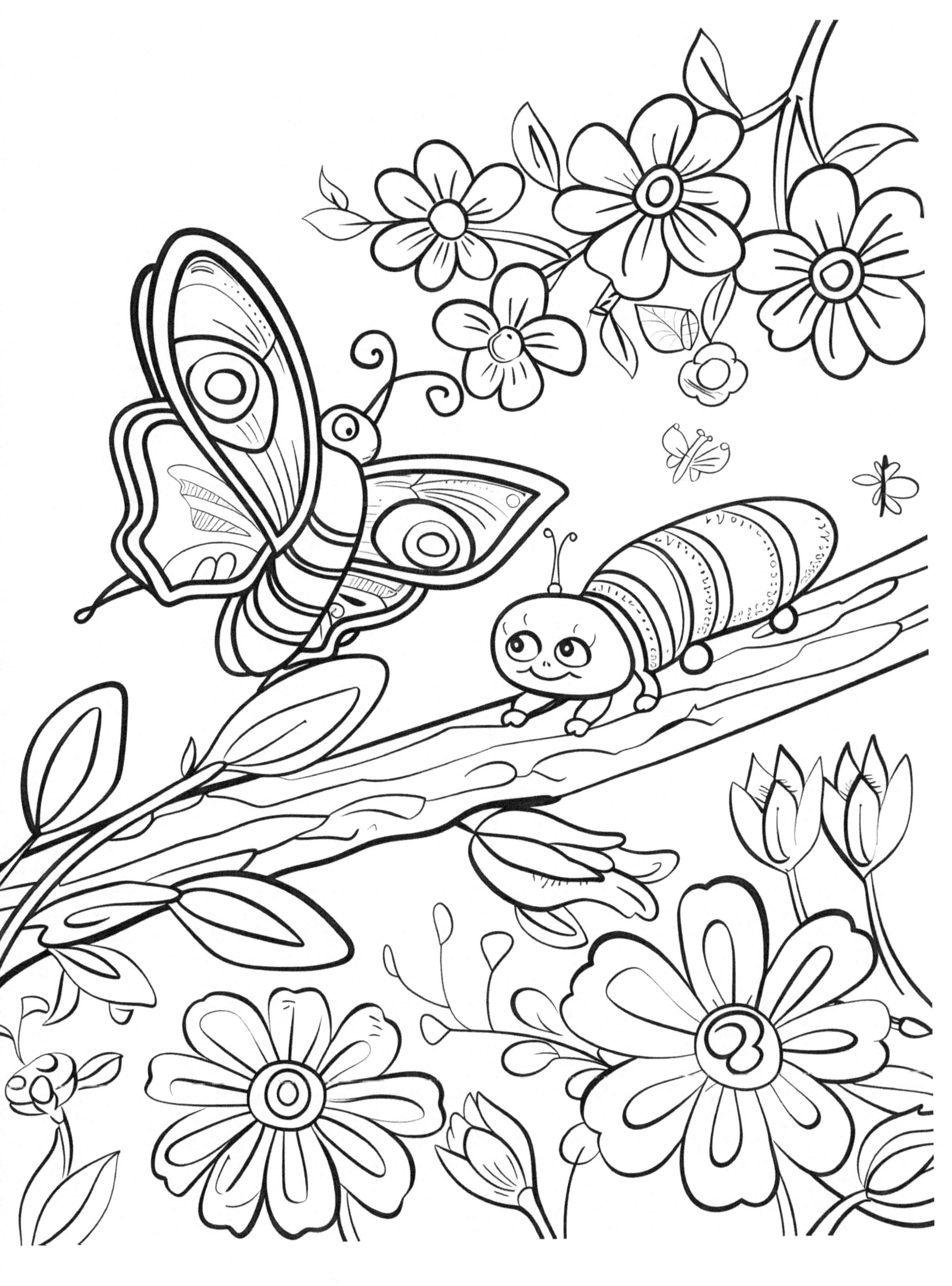

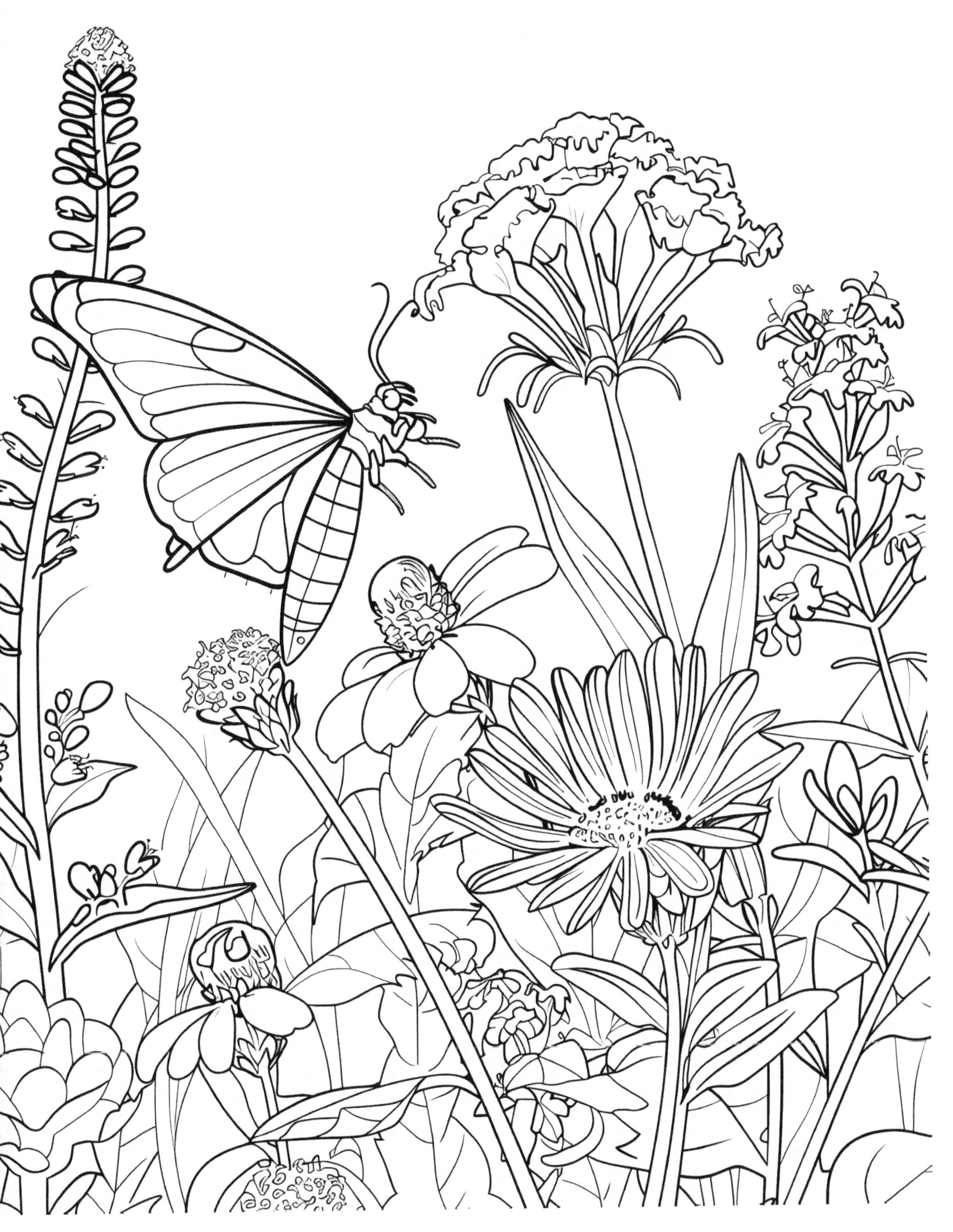

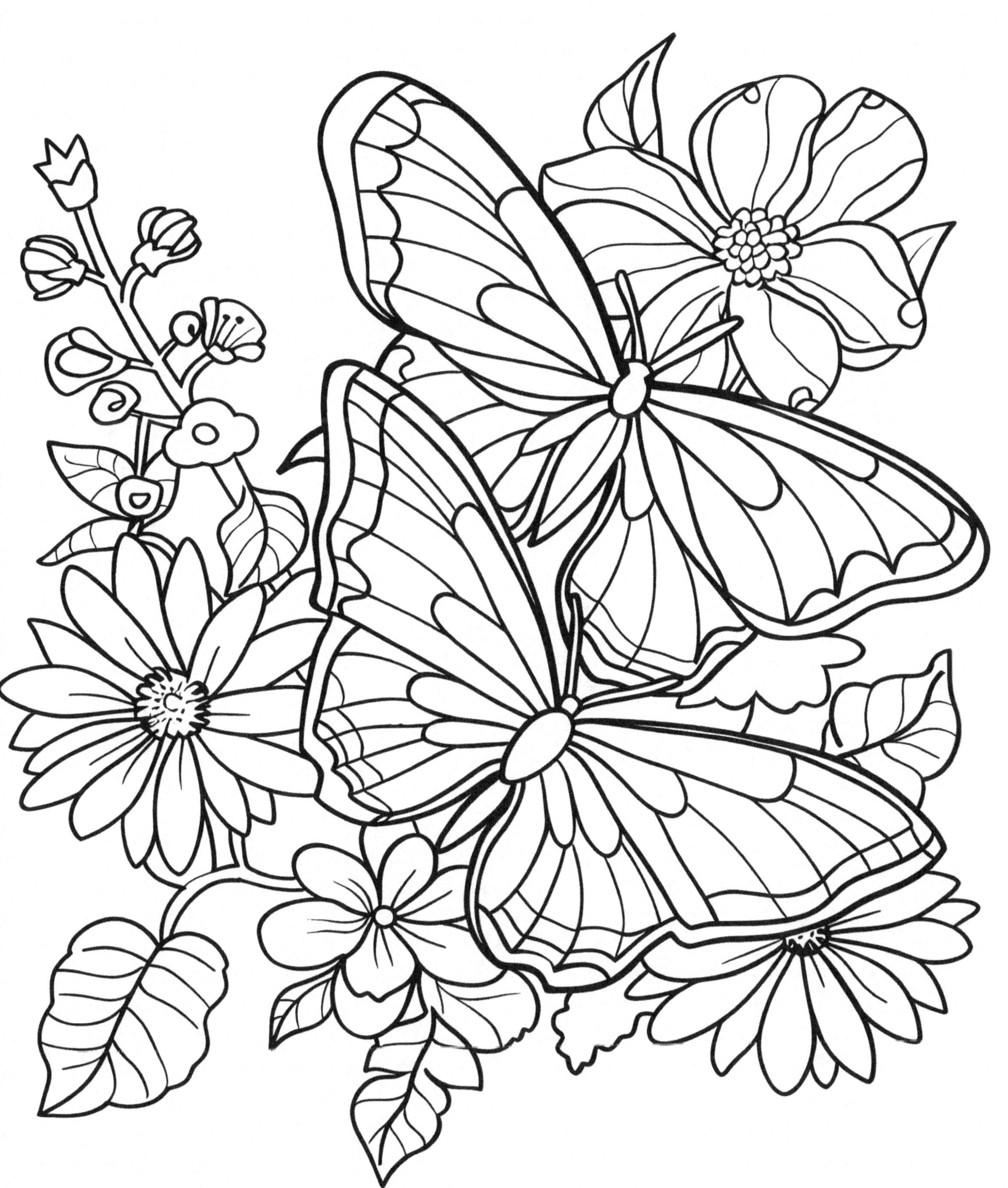

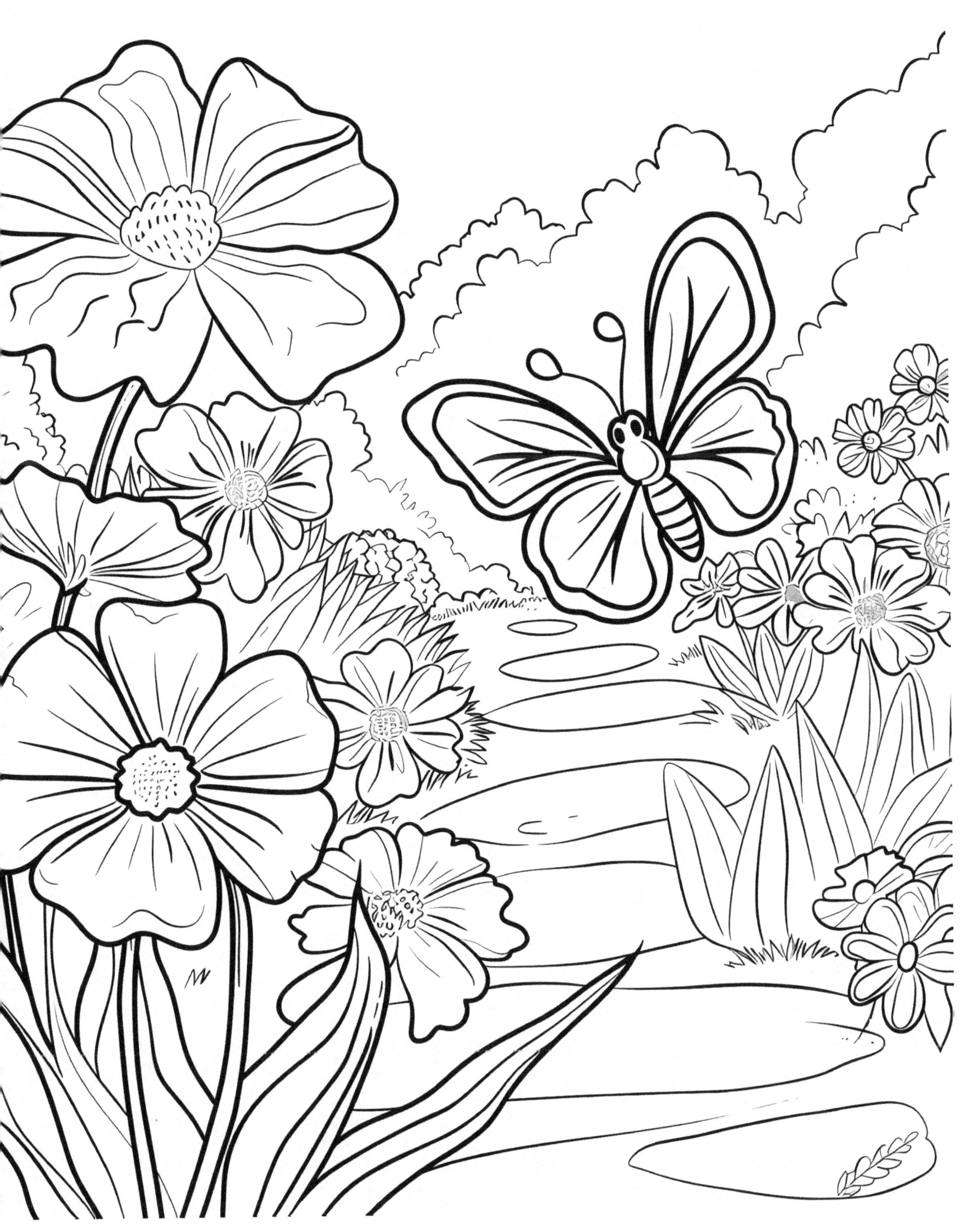

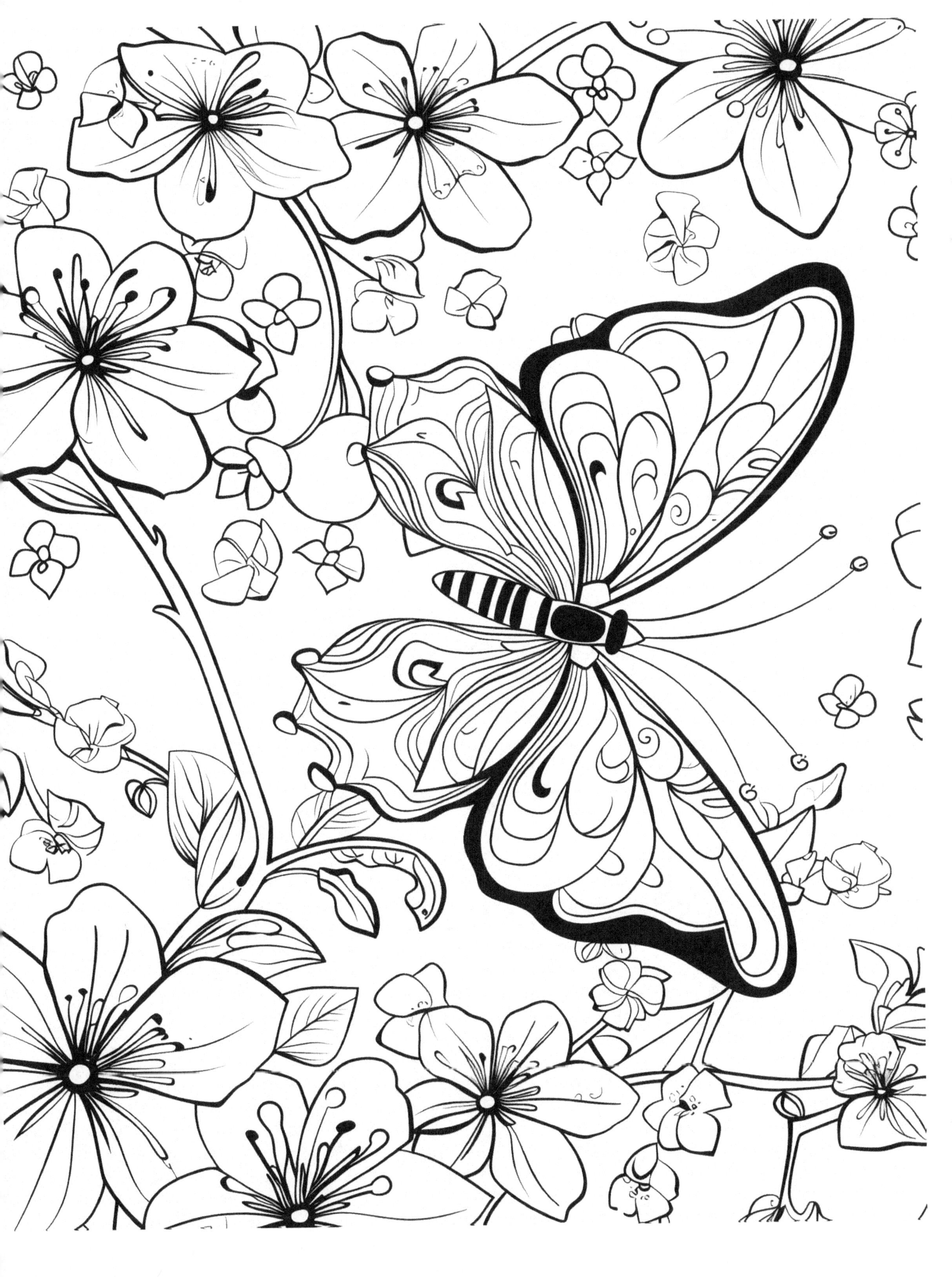

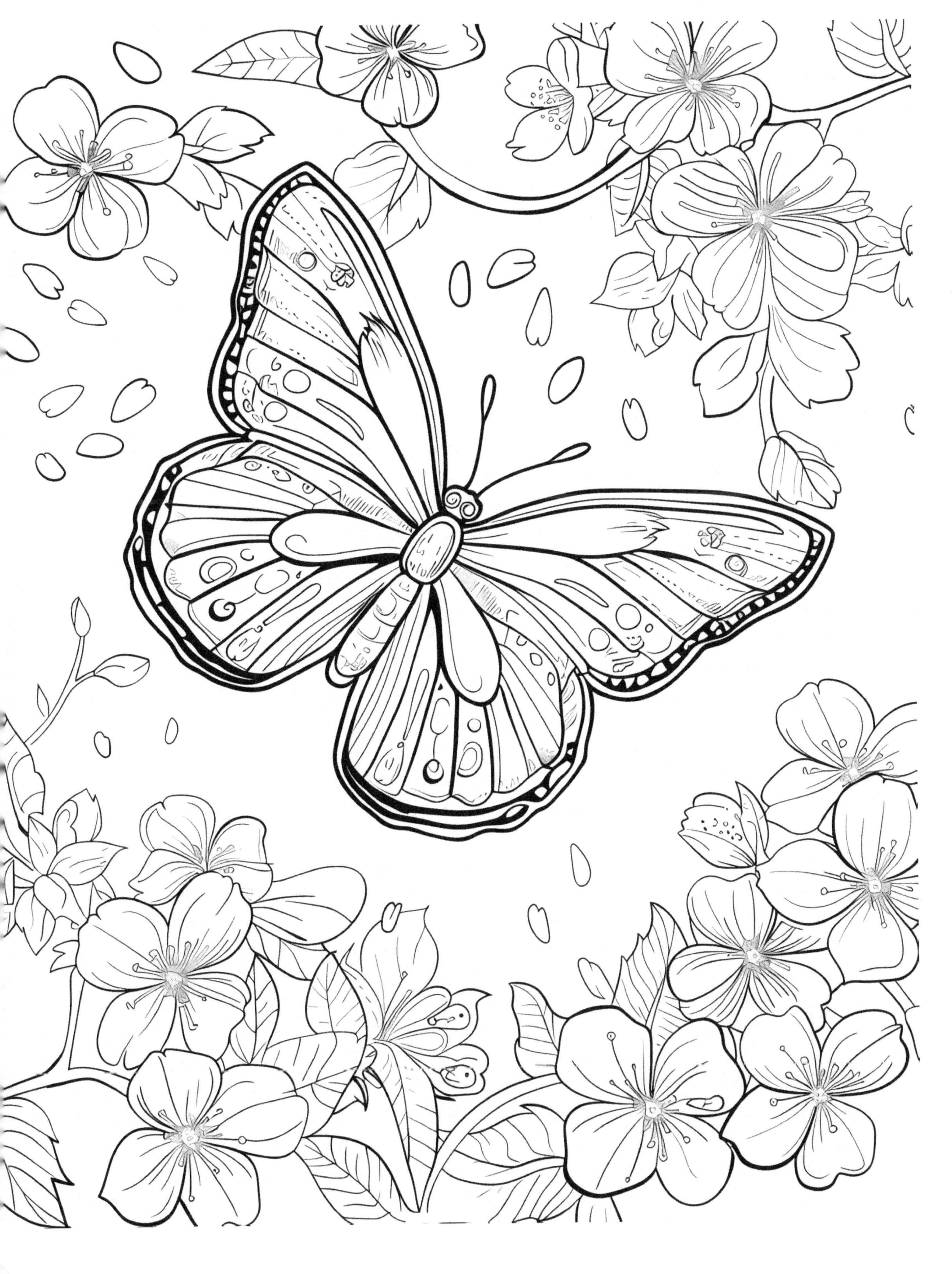

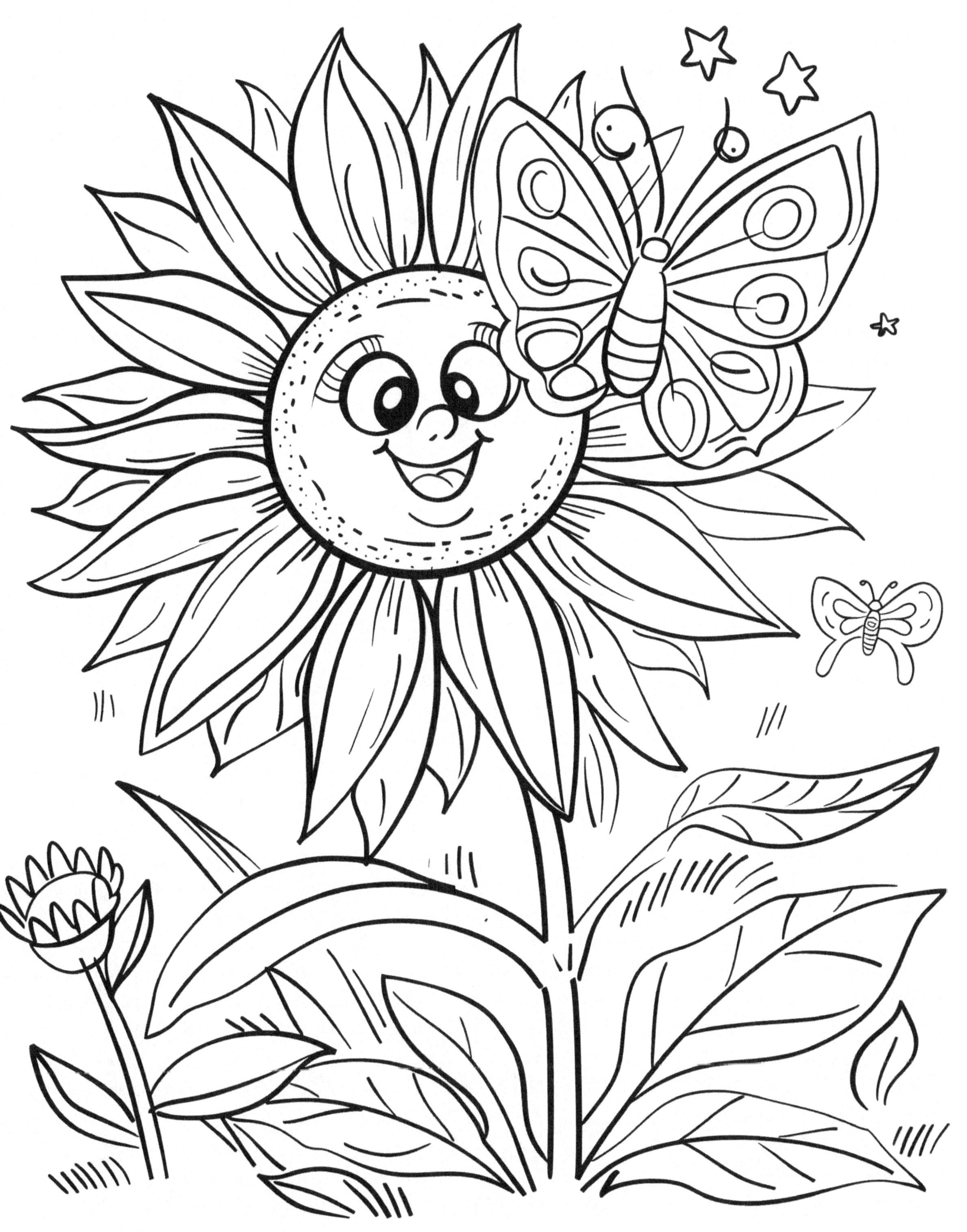

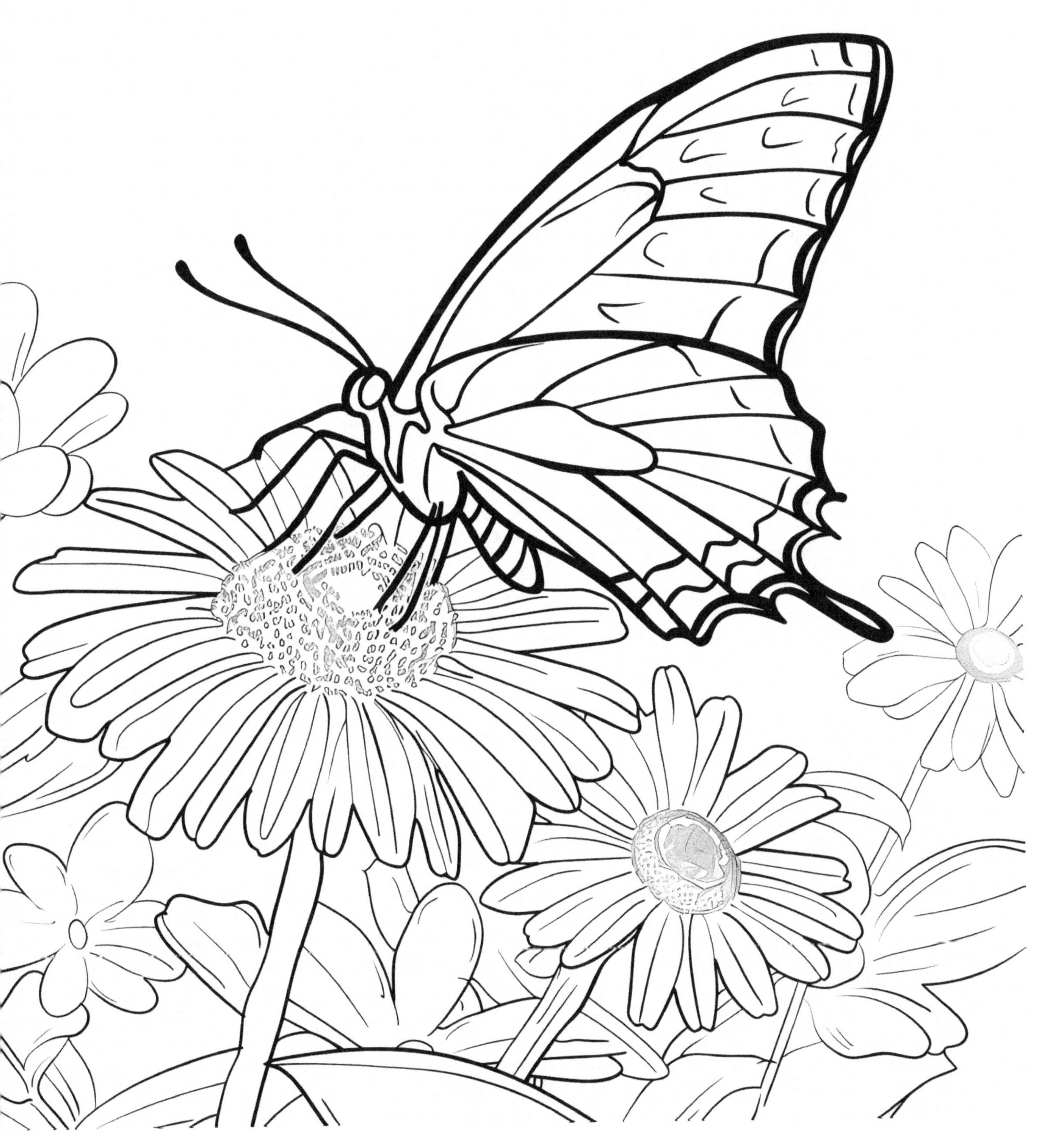

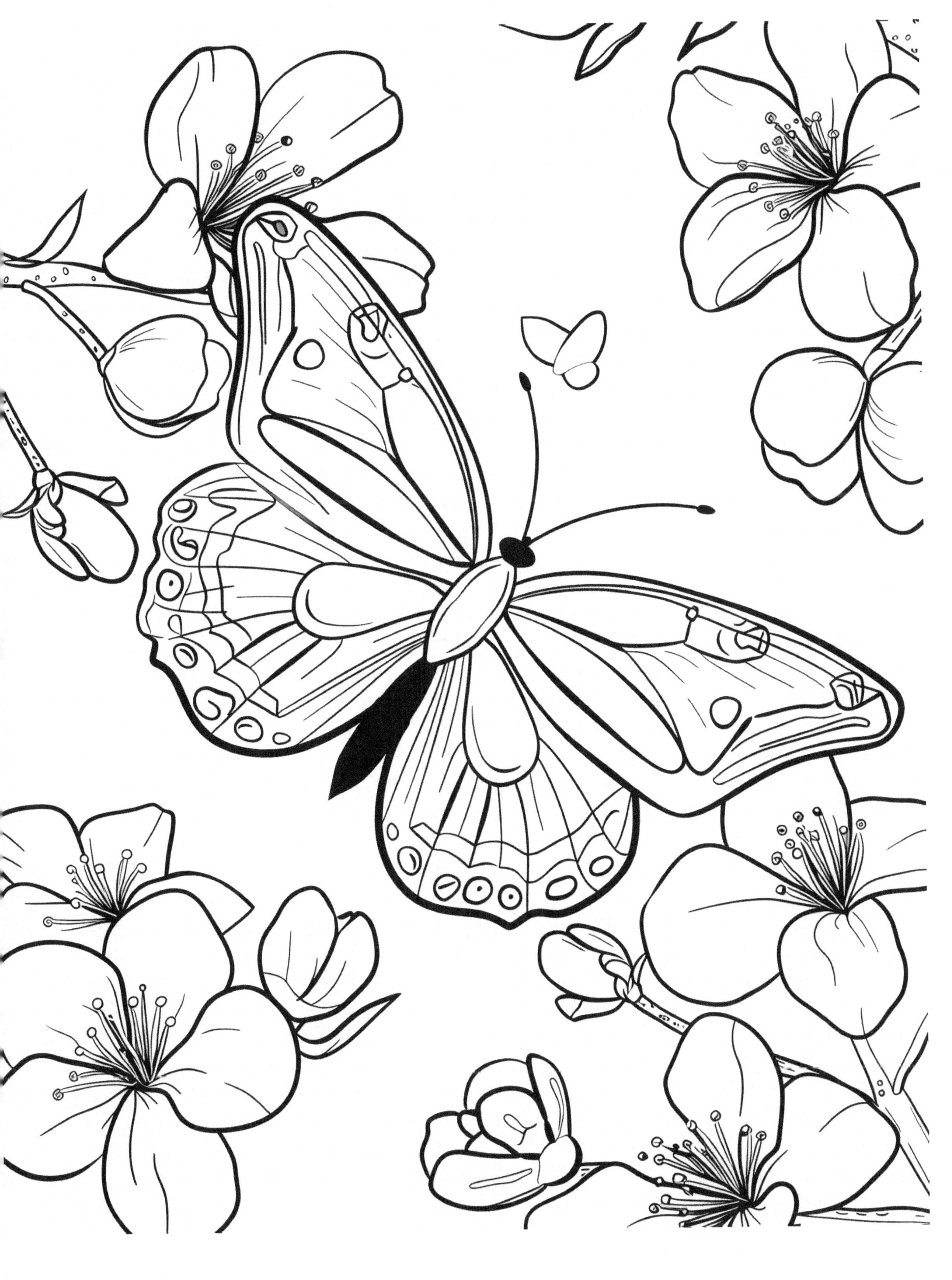

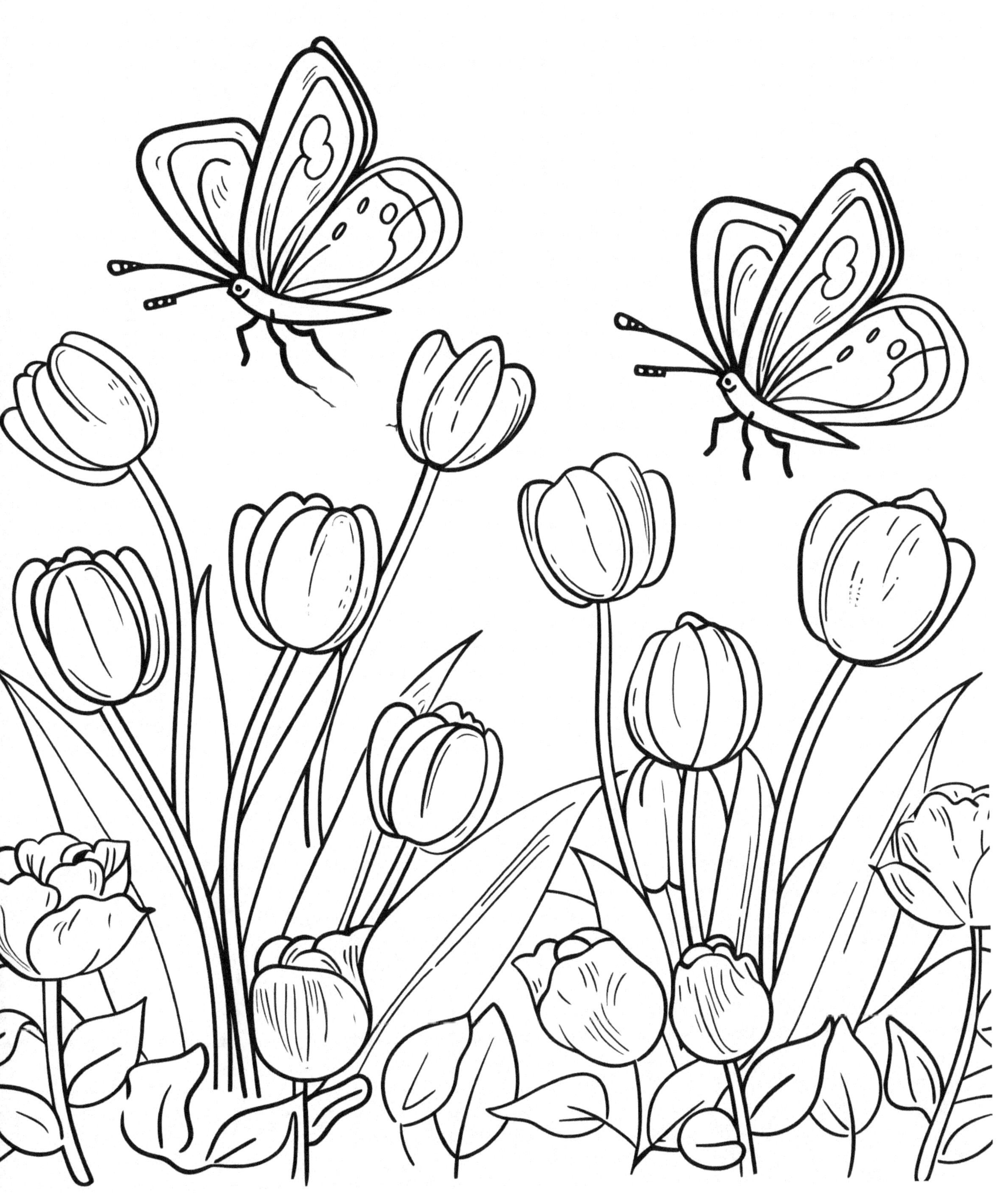

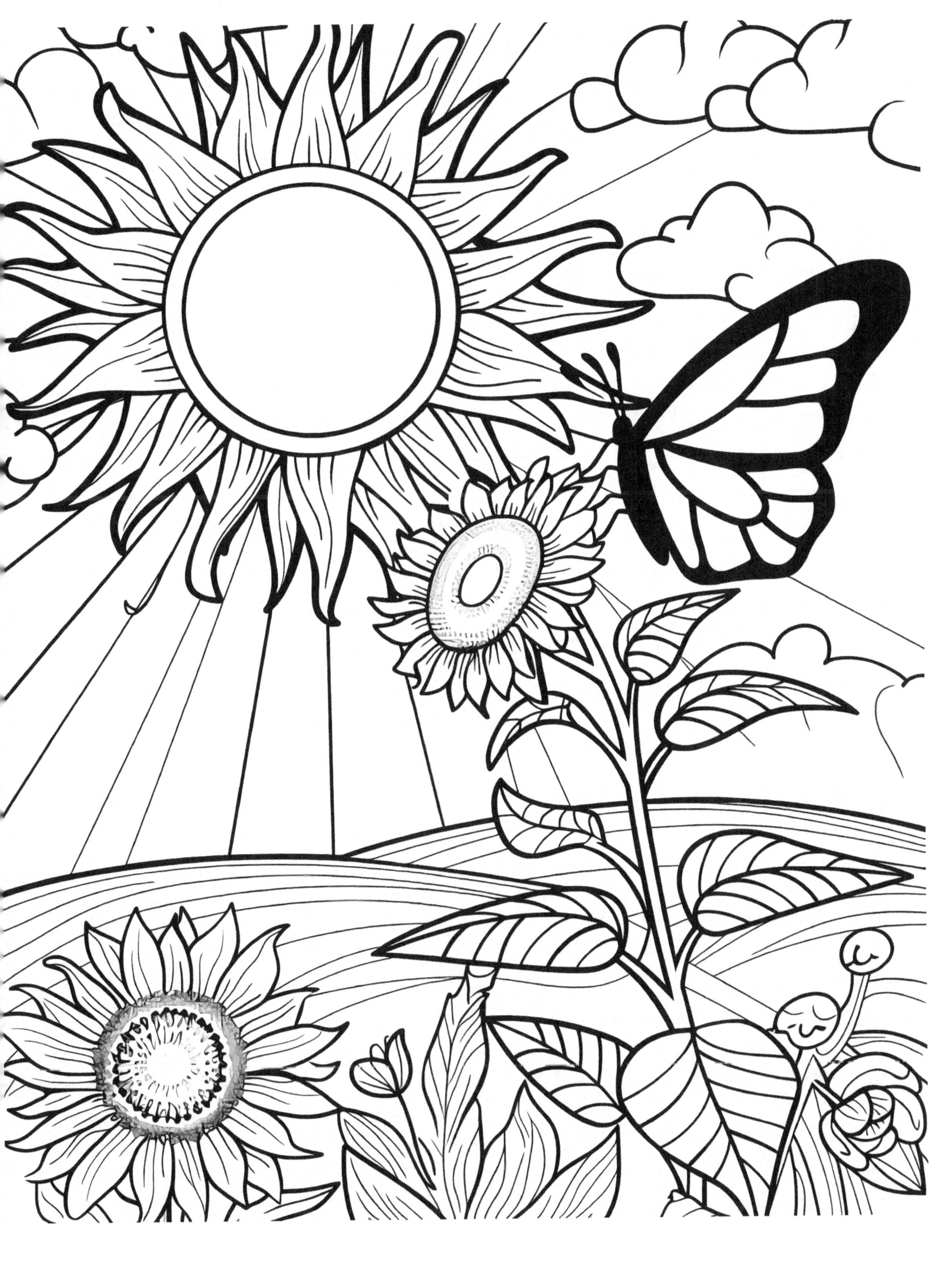

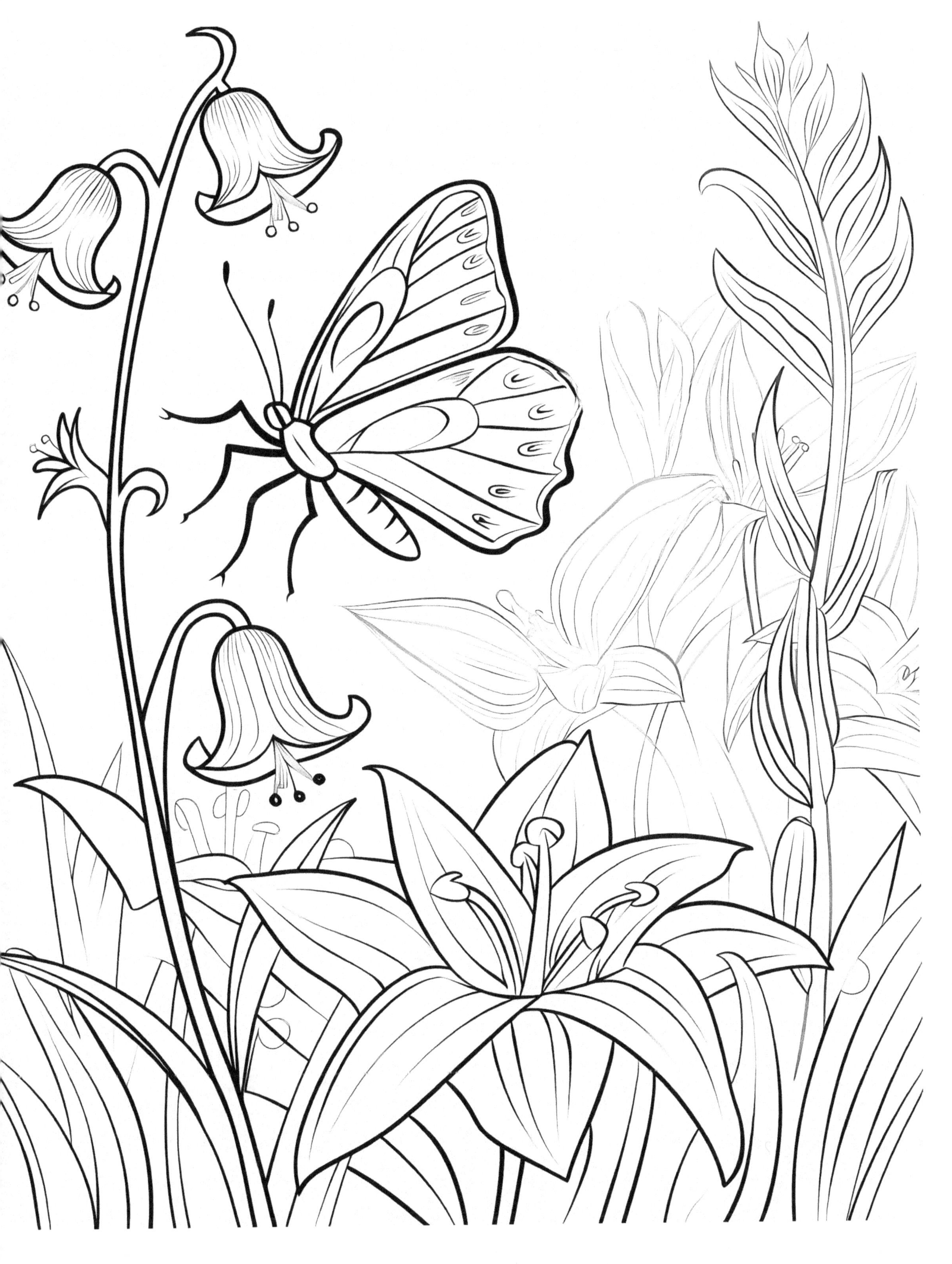

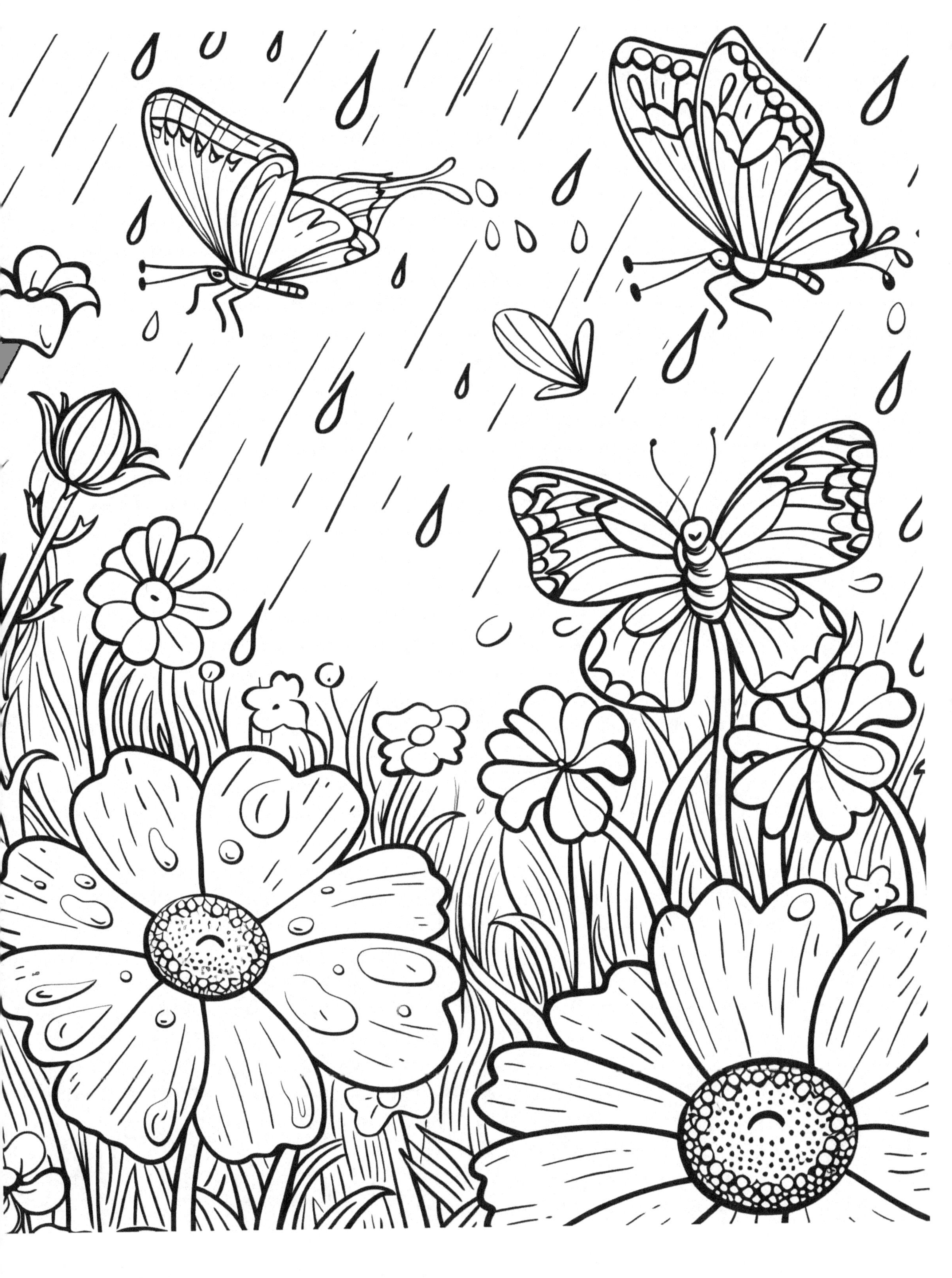

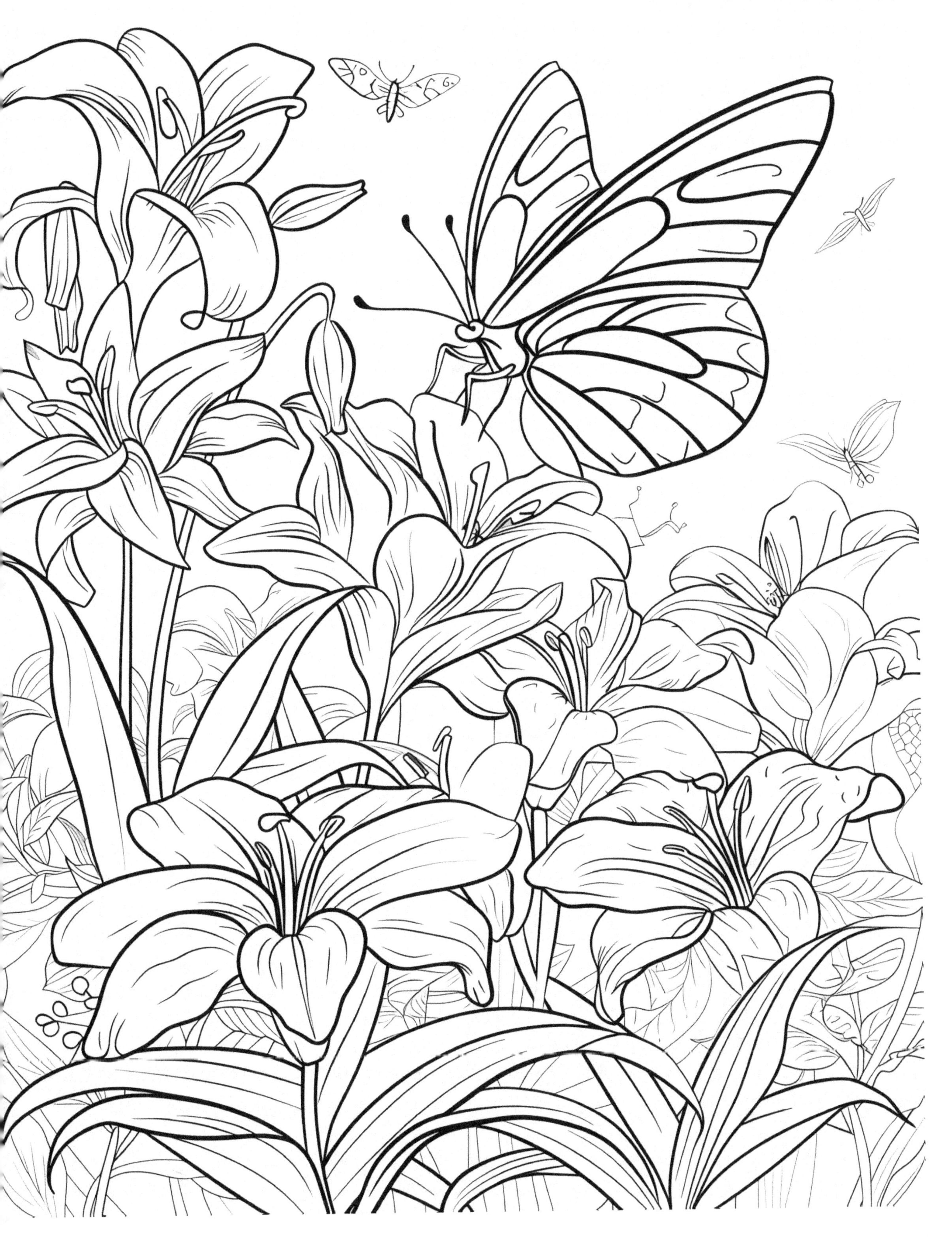

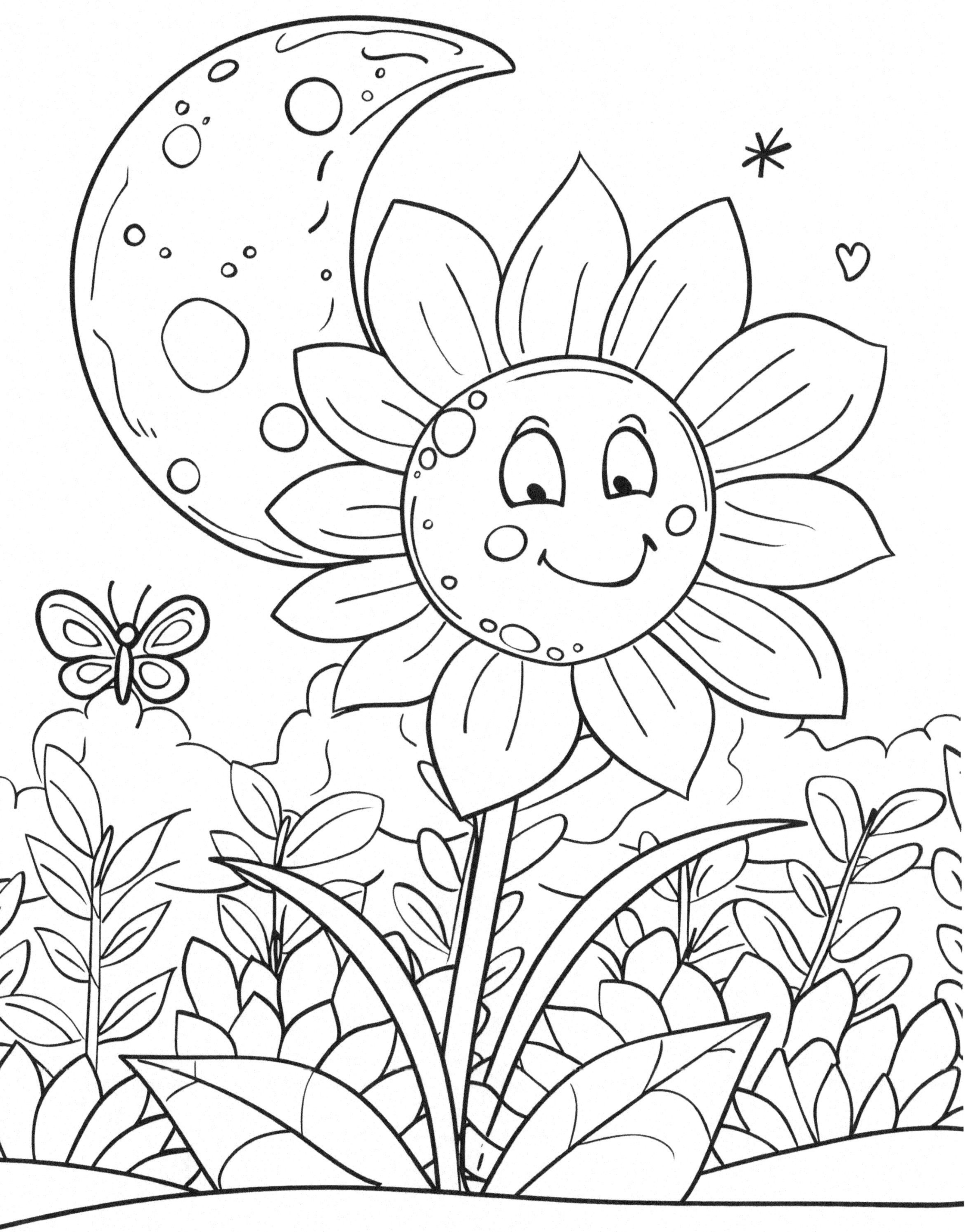

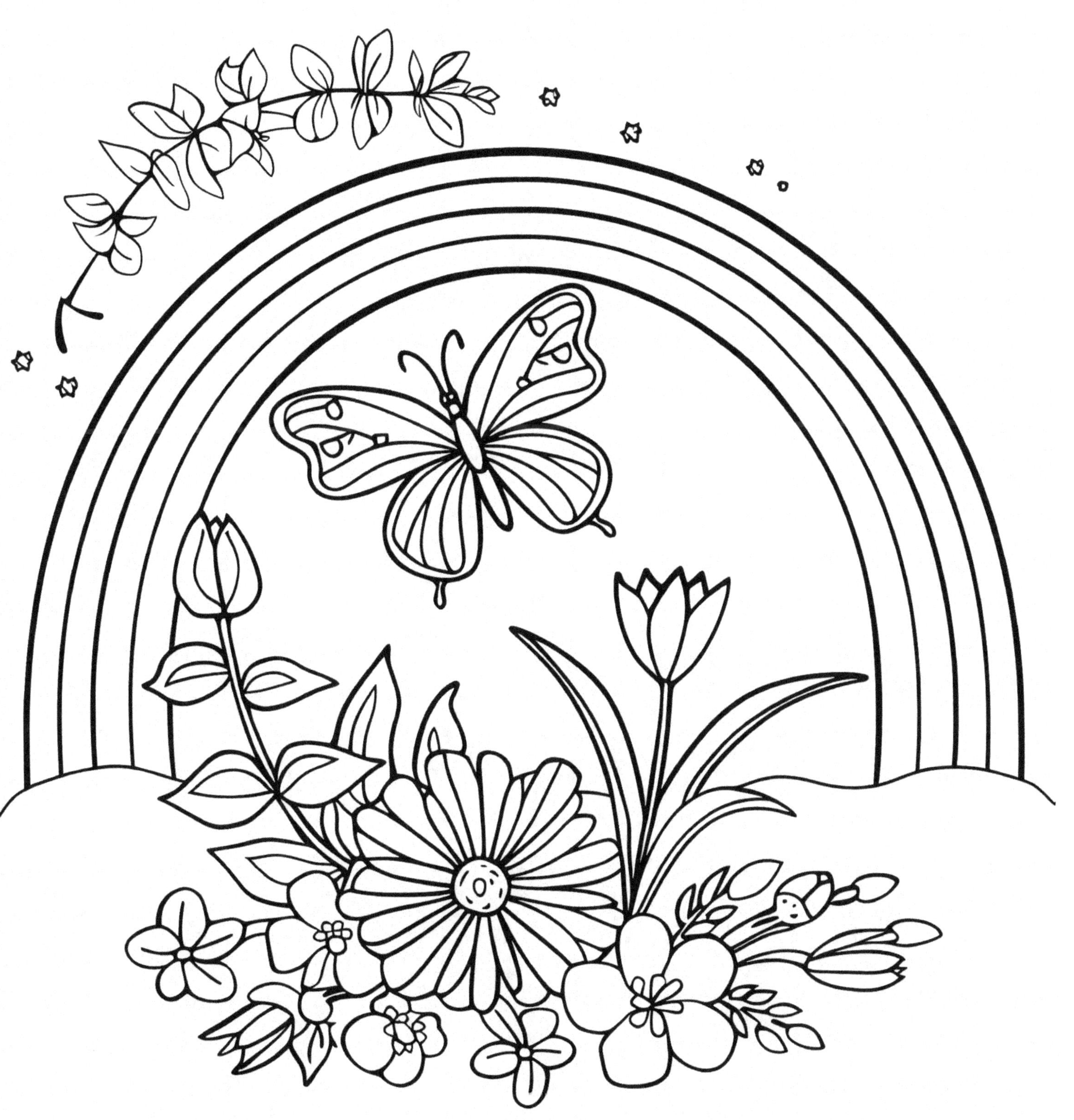

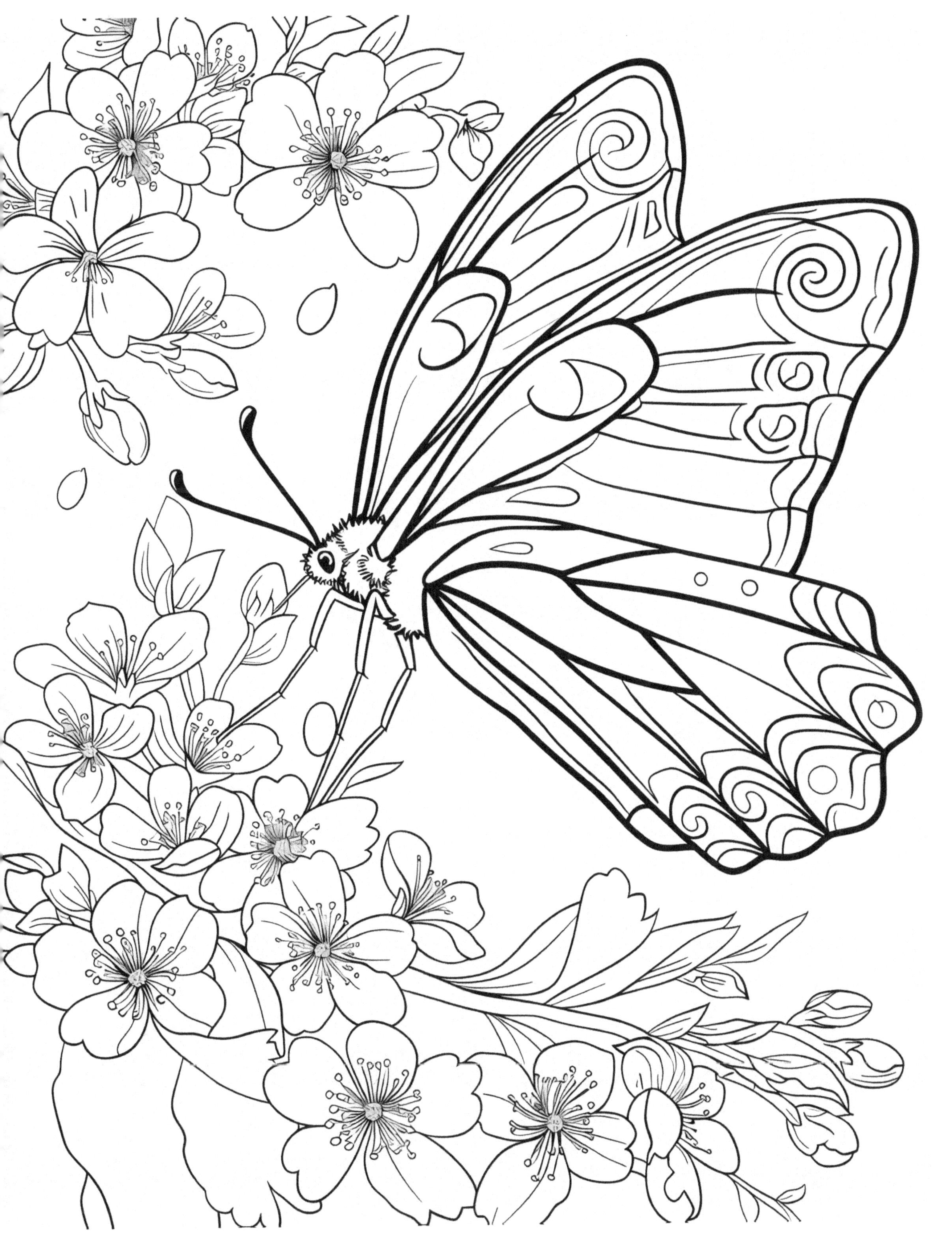

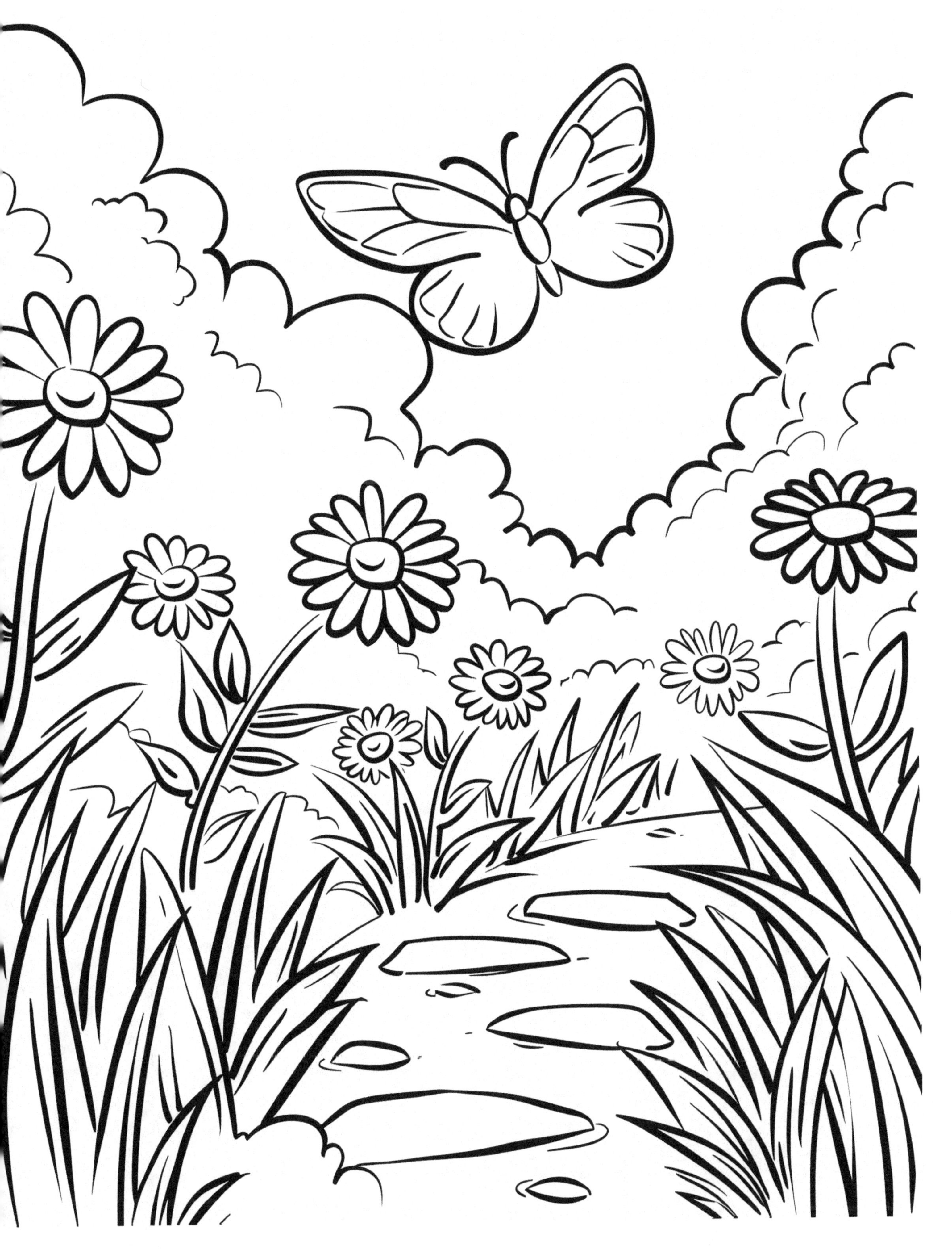

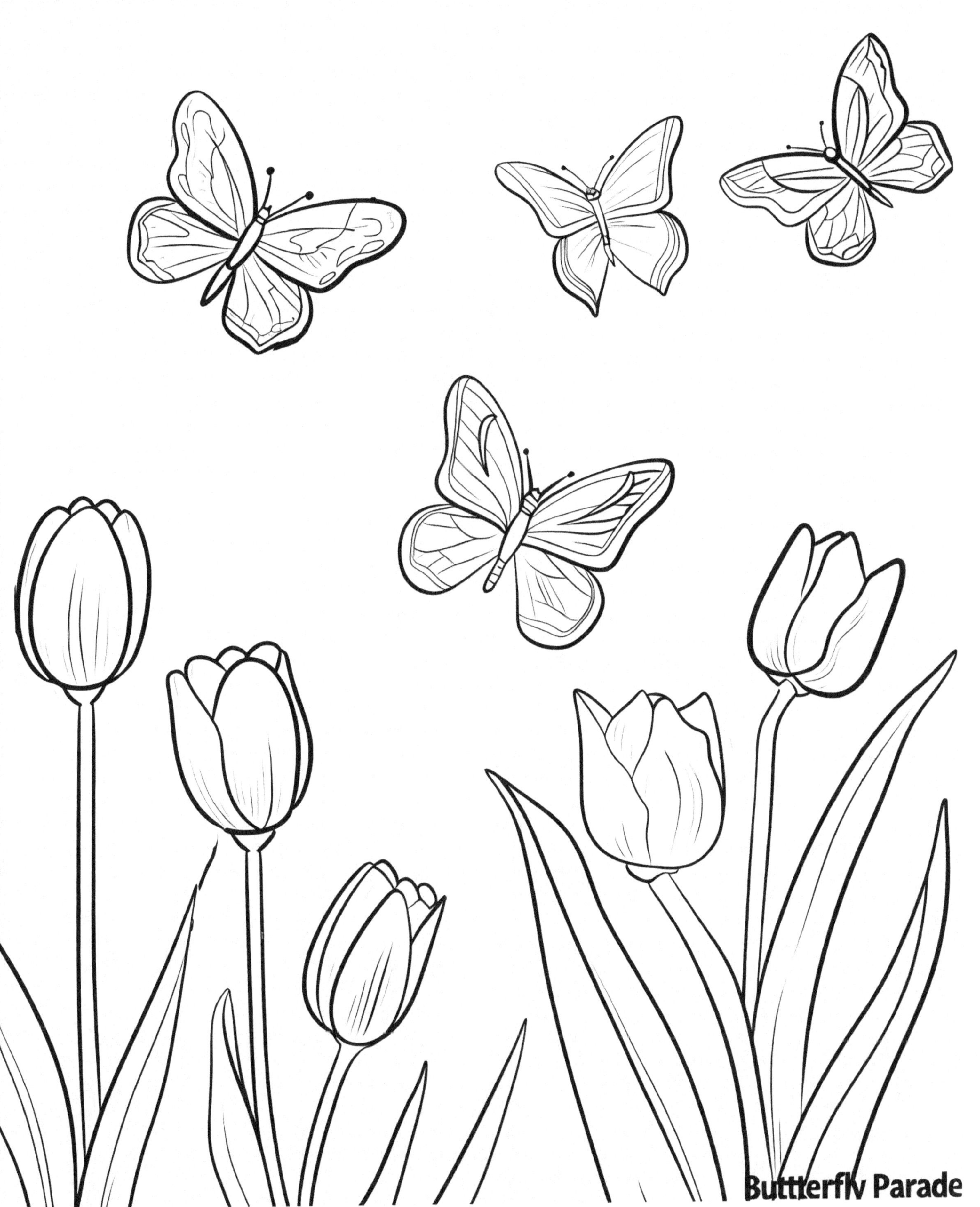
Butterfly Parade

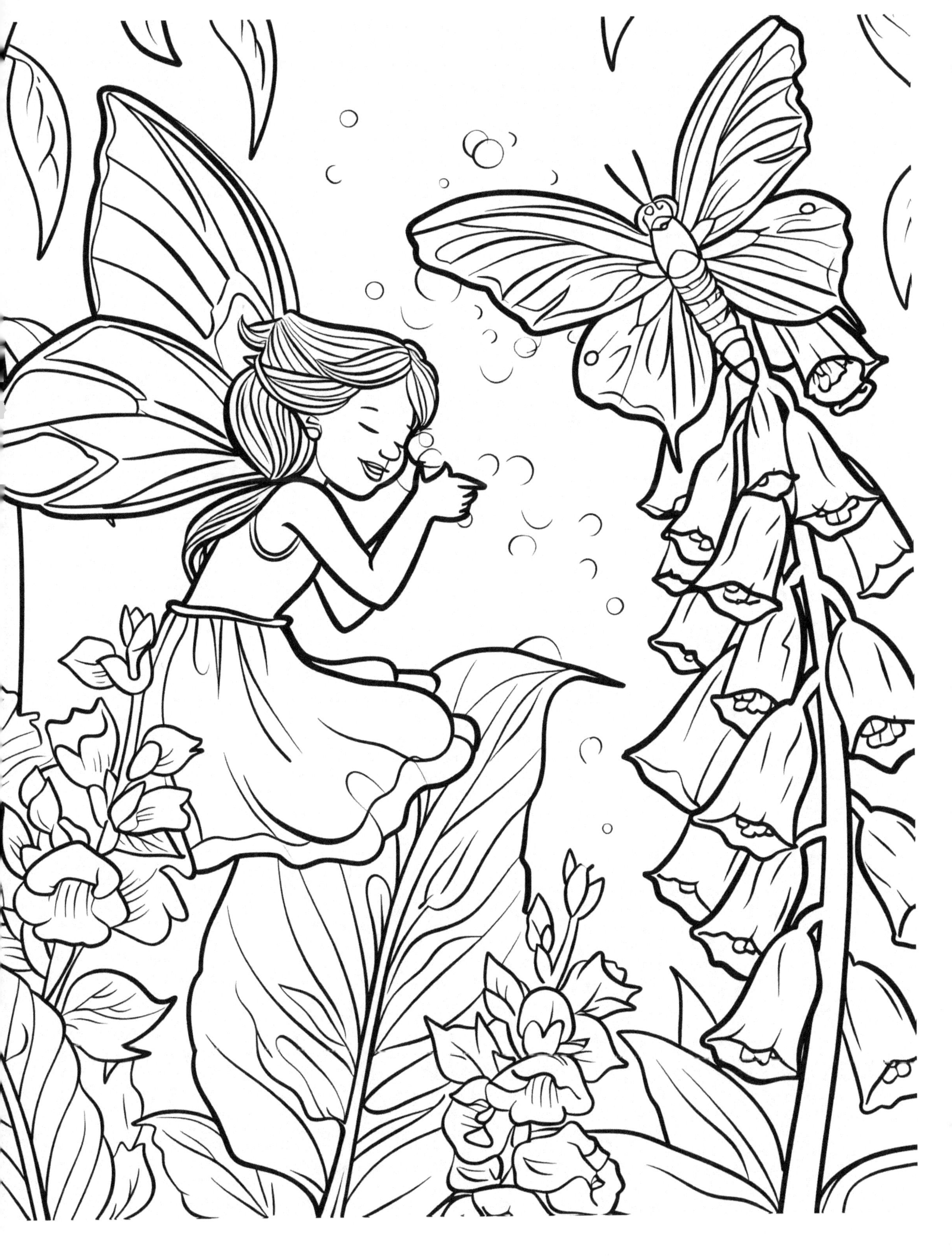